CYNTHIA WHITE

REST
& BUILD

A 31-DAY JOURNEY TO RESTORE YOUR SOUL AND DESIGN A LIFE THAT MATTERS

DocUmeant *Publishing*
244 5th Avenue
Suite G-200
NY, NY 10001
646-233-4366
www.DocUmeantPublishing.com

Published by
DocUmeant Publishing
244 5th Avenue, Suite G-200
NY, NY 10001

646-233-4366

For permission contact the publisher at:
Publisher@DocUmeantPublishing.com

All Scripture quotations, unless otherwise indicated, are taken from the Holy Bible, New International Version®, NIV®. Copyright ©1973, 1978, 1984, 2011 by Biblica, Inc.™ Used by permission of Zondervan. All rights reserved worldwide. www.zondervan.com The "NIV" and "New International Version" are trademarks registered in the United States Patent and Trademark Office by Biblica, Inc.™

Scripture quotations marked "ESV" are taken from The Holy Bible: English Standard Version, copyright 2001, Wheaton: Good News Publishers. Used by permission. All rights reserved.

Scripture quotations marked "NASB" are taken from the New American Standard Bible, Copyright 1960, 1962, 1963, 1971, 1972, 1973, 1975, 1977, 1995 by The Lockman Foundation. Used by permission.

Scripture quotations marked "KJV" are taken from King James Version of the Bible.

Cover & Design by: Ginger Marks
DocUmeant Designs
www.DocUmeantDesings.com

Library of Congress Control Number: 2019937593

ISBN13: 978-1-9378-0199-1 (13.99 USD)

DEDICATION

To my mom and sweet daddy-o, resting in heaven, whose unconditional love has always set my heart at rest.

FOREWORD

I met my friend, Cynthia (Turner) White in her late twenties, at the very start of her venture into full-time Christian work on the staff a global mission organization. We were both serving on the campus of Howard University in Washington, D.C. She joined us at a time when we were already moving forward as a pioneering team but still making new discoveries as to the most effective strategies for primarily reaching students on that prestigious, Historic, African American campus. Cynthia was a treasured addition to the team not only because of her maturity and her career work experience at a sister HBCU in North Carolina, Elizabeth City State University, but also because of her seeking heart to know God and her new marriage to the charismatic young male staff member, James White, that had been a part of the team from its inception in the fall of 1984.

It was my assignment to train and mentor this young woman as a new staff member on the team. I delighted in getting to know her as a friend as we spent time with the team as a whole or just with the other female staff members. We, as staff, and our students had a lot of fun being entertained in their home or attending meetings, retreats and conferences together. As time went by, her high sense of ambition became evident, along with her competence in several areas—including hospitality, speaking and teaching. However, as time unfolded, I observed Cynthia become increasingly at ease with the team, her campus ministry role, with me her trainer and with herself. We and our students began to see the proverbial butterfly escape the cocoon and time has shown the splendid 'butterfly' so many of us admire today, both men and women.

Today there are disciples of Jesus all over the United States, the continent of Africa and elsewhere whose lives have been spiritually touched by this woman of God, directly or indirectly. As a pastor's wife, a mother, Bible teacher and mentor with a sharp mind and discerning spirit, Cynthia has made her mark as a disciple-maker, loyal friend, listener and visionary. She is an entrepreneur who has envisioned and then initiated businesses in the areas of personal branding, image and etiquette consulting, instructor and conference host as well as becoming widely known as a business consultant and conference speaker

Her book is well written, an easy read but substantial in content and instructive as the author weaves her story throughout. Spending thirty-one days in this book, along with The Book [the Bible], will challenge any observing reader to attain a life of R.E.S.T, able to **R**eflect and **R**elease **E**very **S**ituation **T**otally. This is a repeated theme throughout the book. Cynthia writes, "The languishing soul is one that is faint, tired, and weary. But God promises to fill that same soul with good when we look to Him alone. You will find within these pages practical insights and ideas that will help guide you along the path to personal and spiritual maturity, holiness and rest.

Cynthia has sought to be transparent, sharing her personal journey to wholeness and rest. While this is not an exegetical work or theological treatise, it is very Biblically based, effective with poignant personal stories and practical life lessons to be learned for every leader. It is Christ-centered, and sure to connect cross-culturally because the human experience transcends national and ethnic boundaries. However, adjustments can be made for any context. Although designed for women, there are great principles to be gained here and deep encouragement regardless of gender, ethnicity or station in life.

I urge you, the reader, not to skip any of these pages, you may miss her most poignant story and life application. You MUST use an extra pad of paper and pen because there will be plenty of questions on which to muse and you may want to preserve your answers and, as is common in the black church tradition, she "brings it on home" powerfully towards the end. I am so very hopeful that you will find no disappointment here. I wish you a happy and profound, contemplative, reading experience and a life-changing visit with my friend, Cynthia White.

Rev. Marcella L. Charles, M. Div, Pastor
Dorchester Immanuel Church of the Nazarene
Dorchester, MA 02124

ACKNOWLEDGMENTS

Writing and completing this devotional has been one of the hardest things that I have done. And, I'm grateful to God that I didn't have to go at it alone. All of the honor and glory truly belongs to God, my Master Creative Designer.

There are many who helped me with the project by planting and watering encouragement and support. And, I'm eternally grateful for them and the way they too helped shape my "Rest and Build" journey.

First, to my family, I'm thankful for my father, Lambert S. Turner, my "daddy-o", who is resting in heaven and who loved me unconditionally. He taught me how to struggle well in spite of your invisible challenges. And my mother, Nancy W. Turner, my chief prayer warrior, dearest friend, cheerleader, and an evangelist who always reminds me to stay focused. She is truly the epitome of a Remarkable Woman of God.

My husband, Pastor James A. White, who is my rock, best friend, favorite Pastor, Bible teacher and speaker, who has done so much to help make this passion work and ministry a reality. I could not have accomplished this without his prayers, support and willingness to endure many nights of takeout dinners.

My adult children, Christa, Alexis, and Justin, thanks for encouraging, believing in me and giving me the privilege of being your mom and friend.

My tribe, a group of Remarkable Women, who are my "Forever Faithful Friends"–Shelia Kornegay-Davis, Beth McLean,

Diane Tomlinson, Kelli Edwards, Shanera Williamson and Anne White. Your friendship, support, encouragement, and prayers created a desired haven for me to rest and build. My prayer group, of Christian women in leadership, Alisa Bentley, LaToya King, Samantha Kilpatrick, and Bonnie Davis and many others who along the way kept me going with your prayers, encouragement and continued interest in receiving updates on my progress. And lastly to the ladies in my Remarkable Life By Design community, you too pushed me across the finish line. For this, I'm forever grateful.

Throughout this project I have had many editors, but one in particular, Melody Copenny, became my "ram in the bush." Thanks for helping me, with your grace and ease nature, to polish up my devotional by not only making sure that I crossed all of my t's and dotted all of my i's but that my message was clear and consistent.

My love of tea was inspired and cultivated decades ago, by my life-long friend, Sheri Hairston. A cup of tea became a familiar place reminding me to come away and find healing for my soul. This has truly been a journey of recovery that continues to remind me remarkable things happen for the Kingdom when you learn to rest and build.

INTRODUCTION

I was sick and tired of being sick and tired. Medically speaking, I have a condition called Thalassemia, which causes chronic fatigue. But this was different. It was December 2015, I had finished my last speaking event for the year at a women's conference after a grueling schedule. The morning of the event, I was unraveling and imploding emotionally. I felt like I was having a mental breakdown, like I had witnessed in my father several times in my life. I promised God that I would rest if He allowed me to make it through this last assignment. I asked Him to show me how to "rest and build" as Jesus had done, according to the scriptures. Jesus lived a full, meaningful life of ministry that included making time to rest and sleep. He was committed to building God's Kingdom, though exhausting, from a place of REST. This was a lifestyle and leadership model I desperately wanted to follow for the sake of my own well-being. On that day, I promised to take a REST break for what ended up being two years, and I heard God's promise to rebuild my life.

How did I get here? I had been dealing with stress from my ministry and the demands of my business development along with bouts of insomnia and anxiety for several years. Unknown to most, my anxiety was starting to rule my life. For the first time in my medical history I was experiencing issues with an elevated blood pressure. My doctor was considering medication.

According to an article by Elizabeth Scott on VeryWellMind. com, *"People who are chronically sleep deprived are nine times more likely to show depression symptoms and 17 times more likely to show anxiety symptoms. Research has shown that a lack of sleep ramps up your stress response so that you are much more likely to view normal behavior as a threat."*

As a business owner who coaches, mentors, and speaks on leadership presence and personal brand strategy—while starting another business advocating for woman to live their best lives with grace and ease—what I was attempting to build was in jeopardy. I was struggling to keep all of my many priorities in order. As a leader in ministry and business, clinically diagnosed with attention deficit disorder (ADD), dyslexia, and an anxiety disorder, I could not afford to ignore my own mental health challenges. I needed to slow down, scale back, and learn how to REST.

Also, I was tired of failing myself! As a pastor's wife and ministry leader for more than 31 years, I needed rest from the tears, tugs, trials and traumas to my heart and soul in my effort to love and care for people in need. I have learned that depression is real, even for church leaders. Self-care is necessary and a remarkable thing. It was time for me to slow down and love myself better, for the sake of the Kingdom of God and for my own sake.

God allowed me to make it through my message that day without crashing and burning. I witnessed Him do exceedingly and abundantly more than I could ask for or even think about.

I knew that if I made it to the other side of that speaking event, I was never coming back to this life of hurrying, busily creating, feeling overwhelmed, and being committed beyond capacity.

It wasn't the life that I was designed to live. As I began to look over my life, I realized that for most of my Christian life I have been on a search to find my "Garden of Eden." It's the place where life created by God is enjoyed in His presence . . . connected, fruitful, productive, and unhurried. Imagine walking and talking with God, and working diligently, but not by the "sweat of your brow". How sweet and pleasant this would be.

I knew that I was created to live and lead a high-impact life, but this busy life of living in the fast lane was taking me down a path that compromised my clarity, business, reputation, and ministry effectiveness as a leader.

What's your "rest and build story"? Are you tired of living in the fast lane of a high impact life while trying to create a pulled together life and image even though, on the inside, you are about to crash?

This devotional is designed to help you, as a leader, build an even better life by making the time to rest deliberately and embrace stillness in God in the midst of overwhelming obstacles and opposition. Move away from the constant hurry, stress, and frustration to a place of peace, joy, and fulfillment. Find calm amidst the chaos and watch Him restore your life and lead you to lasting change by learning to REST and build. You deserve to design and live a life that matters without wearing yourself out to do so.

Come, let us have some tea and continue to talk about happy things. –Chaim Potok

I believe that some lessons are best learned over a cup of hot tea. Pour yourself a cup of tea and let's begin this Rest and Build journey together. Daily, I will share a scripture that talks about rest and ways to connect to our lives. And in the same naked and not ashamed way that Genesis 2:25 talks about, with transparency I will share parts of my story in hopes of helping other women find the courage to rest . . . contemplate, create, celebrate, and contribute. Find ways daily, through the reflection questions, quotes, prayer, practical suggestions and self-care tips to get the most out of your 31-day journey.

Lastly, I cannot talk about rest without addressing the importance of sleep. Throughout this devotional, I will share nuggets for restful sleep, to help you improve your sleep hygiene.

Be still. Breathe deeply. Let's get started.

Nuggets for Restful Sleep: Sleep is a Gift from God

Imagine if there were no sleep. Some are tantalized by the thought, speculating that they would be even more productive because the elimination of sleep would enable them to reach their full potential. Others are attracted to the idea of a life without sleep because it would make the party last longer, opening up vast opportunities to have more fun.

The truth, however, is that a sleepless life would be a life of bondage. We would become slaves to our work, for our labor would have no end.

"By the seventh day God had finished the work he had been doing; so on the seventh day he rested from all his work" (Genesis 2:2).

God rested because He had finished His work, and He gave us the Sabbath so that we could enter His rest each week.

In essence, sleep is like a nightly Sabbath, a much-needed opportunity to rest from our labor, to cast aside the cares and worries of our day and to renew the body and mind.

"In vain you rise early and stay up late, toiling for food to eat—for he grants sleep to those he loves" (Psalm 127:2).

DAY 1: BUILD A LIFE OF CONTEMPLATION

"There is something in the nature of tea that leads us into a world of quiet contemplation of life."
–Lin Yutang

"Thus the heavens and the earth were finished, and all the host of them. And on the seventh day God finished his work that he had done, and he rested on the seventh day from all his work that he had done. So God blessed the seventh day and made it holy, because on it God rested from all his work that he had done in creation." (Genesis 2:1-3 ESV).

Contemplation. When you hear the word, what ideas and thoughts roll through your mind? What sounds do you hear? How does it make you feel? What impressions are made?

Contemplation is the ability to break free, invite calm into your life, and allow your mind and heart to actively rest in God intentionally focusing and connecting with Him from your soul. It's a time to focus on being rather than doing in order to nourish and restore your soul as you meditate on His works. Unfortunately, this is a lost art in today's fast-paced world, one filled with exhausting activities and tasks that rule our lives and enslave us.

Imagine this: Rest. Slowing life down and doing absolutely NOTHING. Tap into the Spirit so that you can purposefully reflect and observe your life while connecting your true best self to God. This is the LIFE! The Remarkable Life for which you were made.

On the seventh day, God paused and rested. This was a special time that He set apart and blessed. The word *blessed* implies being in a happy state of mind. And He called this special blessed period of rest the *Sabbath*.

After completing all that He had created, God, Elohim, the all-powerful Creator, paused to contemplate and celebrate. He knew that this contribution to the world would uniquely deliver value and make this empty world a better place. And He declared it indeed to be a very good thing! What a picture of the Remarkable Life by design in action.

REST—a rest from within the depths of the soul allows you to avoid being overwhelmed by burnout and breakdown. This type of rest brings safety as it moves you towards contemplation which brings greater clarity.

For much of my life, this was the road not traveled. I feared it because I didn't want to be seen as lazy, unproductive, or lacking potential. I hurriedly moved from activity to activity and adversity to adversity with little regard for the damage it was doing to me spiritually, physically, and emotionally. I needed an extended time to rest, restore, and refocus.

As women, we were designed by God to be life-givers. But, like me, most of us are afraid to slow down, calm our lives, and be still. REST. Contemplate.

Imagine the life you were designed to live compared to the one you are building for yourself at the moment that is simply destroying you, exhausting you, or leaving you feeling unfilled. Is it really worth it?

I believe that we all want to live a Remarkable Life—full, meaningful, and lacking absolutely nothing—as described in John 10:10. We want our lives to matter! Perhaps the real problem is that we are afraid to slow down, lean in and look in deeper. We don't want to come face-to-face with our fears, disappointments, and repressed guilt over the less than Remarkable Life we have chosen to live in secret (despite our seemingly happy pictures on social media).

What if I could take you back to the beginning, to the original blueprint? What if you could experience life as intended by the Master Creative Designer—God? Imagine building and living a creative, fulfilling and fruitful life through rest.

And through the power of a deeper rest, a soul rest, you could contemplate, create, and celebrate a life that contributes a unique promise of value that is truly remarkable—a life of influence and impact "worth the remark!"

It would be rather arrogant to think that we are brilliant enough to come up with this kind of life ourselves. So, we must rely on the blueprint for the Remarkable Life found in God's spoken Word, the Bible.

In Genesis, we see from the beginning that God not only created rest, but He Himself rested.

Life is best lived and understood through the gift of soul R.E.S.T.

My hope and prayer is that you will do the work of soul rest by carving out less than 30 minutes a day over the next 31 days to R.E.S.T. and build.

R.E.S.T.: Release Every Situation Totally to God

Schedule a date with Him over a cup of tea—our power drink for soul rest. It is our symbol that reminds us to rest. Sip and savor the moment! Think deeply about the life of purposeful impact you want to design and build. Allow the Holy Spirit to move you from a crowded life to a place of calm. Choose to build from a place of rest. With grace and ease, seize the moment and make it happen!

Reflect and Release Every Situation Totally

1. Would you say that your life is restful?
2. How would your life change if you lead and acted from a place of soul rest?
3. What is one thing you'd like to see change over the next 31 days?

Tea Time and Conversation with God

Lord, show me how to imitate You by honoring the Sabbath. Like You, I want to rest and build a life filled with contemplation, celebration, creation, and contribution. Teach me to rest in You. And teach me what it means in Matthew 11:29–30 that your burden is easy and your yoke is light. I'm tired of too often being busy and feeling overwhelmed and burned out. I need the rest and soul refreshment that You provide. Please let me experience that today. I choose to Release Every Situation Totally to You. In Jesus' name, Amen.

Activate and Restfully Make It Happen

What we plant in the soil of contemplation, we shall reap in the harvest of action. —Meister Eckhart

Take five minutes to simply ponder the word "rest." Do the same with the word "Sabbath."

- What does each word mean to you?
- What does a restful life look like?
- What activities do you associate with rest?
- How can you keep the Sabbath in today's busy world?
- What activities come to mind when you think about hurry?

Consider the kind of life you desire to design and build. What will you need to do differently to invite REST into your life? What resources will you need? Lastly, create a Sabbath Day basket with items (candles, tea, planner, puzzles, coloring books, a journal, fuzzy socks, essential oils, etc.) to use for your REST breaks throughout this 31-day devotional.

Restful Sleep: Sleep is Part of the Rhythm of Life

Each of us spends nearly one-third of our life asleep. This process is as natural, and as rhythmic as the rising and setting of the sun. The body has circadian rhythms that act as a timing system, helping to regulate sleep and wakefulness.[1] These circadian rhythms closely follow the daily cycle of light and darkness.

External timing cues, such as the fall of darkness and the drop in temperature at nighttime, act as sleep signals for your body. Similarly, the light of dawn and the rise in temperature are signals that promote alertness. These cues help "set" the time of your body's circadian clock.

When we disrupt this rhythm, by sleeping in much later on weekends than we do during the workweek, we throw off the timing of our body clock. As a result, we may feel sluggish and groggy during the day when we should be alert, and alert at night when we should feel sleepy.

This misalignment, resulting from sleep restriction during the workweek and catch-up sleep on weekends, has been called "social jetlag".[2] One of the keys to healthy sleep is to maintain a consistent sleep schedule, going to bed early enough to allow at least seven hours of sleep and waking up around the same time each day.

———————　꙳⟨◊⟩꙳　———————

Self-Care Task: Get a facial or massage and release your stress.

———————

DAY 2: BUILD A LIFE OF ABIDING

Tea time is a chance to slow down, pull back and appreciate our surroundings. —Letitia Baldrige

"Come to me, all who labor and are heavy laden, and I will give you rest" (Matthew 11:28 ESV).

*G*rowing up, I learned from watching my parents that life can be difficult, stressful, and troubled by cares and afflictions. I saw that they, like many of us, came to expect that work should make them tired and weary.

Indeed, our society *encourages* us to work ourselves almost to the point of exhaustion. Like many of you, I assumed juggling many tasks and staying up working into the wee hours were prerequisites to success.

Yet God, our Creative Master Designer, offers a way for us to restfully push through the stress and beyond our breaking point. Jesus is extending the greatest invitation. Come to Him and find rest.

I believe that we were made to find joy and pleasure in our work, but not without Him. Work was designed to be done as a form of worship to God. And when we find ourselves weighed down, worn out and weary trying to build a life for ourselves and our families, that doesn't look or feel like worship. We can work with grace and ease when the going gets tough if we learn to rest, wholeheartedly, and from the soul.

Do the responsibilities of business, ministry, family, or career leave you feeling heavy-laden? Do you feel like you are sinking under the weight and pressures of life?

Perhaps you need a "come to Jesus" moment. He has extended the invitation. Stop hustling and grinding. Align yourself to God's purpose and plan. Cease from constantly moving. Pause and REST. Wholehearted soul rest allows you to connect with Jesus and give Him your weights and burdens in life. He also wants to show us how to rest, in our work, while leaning on Him.

The Remarkable Life is full of peace and comfort. It's meant to be lived well, in the midst of burdens, burnouts, and breakdowns, enjoyed in the presence of the God of Peace. He is the Lord of rest and a burden-bearer who is our ever-present help.

When you think of the Remarkable Life you are seeking to design and build, intentionally choose to not take on unnecessary stress. Instead, REST. From your soul, abide in Christ and believe that He has the power to carry your burdens.

It takes a Remarkable Woman who has the courage to build a stress-free life filled with deliberate rest, because she has learned to come to Jesus and lean on Him totally. Regardless of the things weighing you down, stay connected with Him and REST.

Reflect and Release Every Situation Totally

1. What long-held assumptions do you have about work and rest?
2. Where do these ideas come from?
3. How is your connection with Jesus shaping the way you live?

Tea Time and Conversation with God

Lord, forgive me for living a hurried, stressful life. I know You have much better things for me. You have still waters and green pastures. You have peace and prosperity. Just as Jesus took time away from the hustle and bustle to rest, please teach me to do the same. In Jesus' name, Amen.

Activate and Restfully Make It Happen

"A life of rest and peace in God is good; a life of pain lived in patience is still better; but to have peace in a life of pain is best of all." —Meister Eckhart

In your journal, make a list of your burdens. Symbolically, lift the list up to heaven as a way of reminding yourself that God is lovingly lifting your burdens off of you.

Feeling exhausted? Take a power nap! Just 10 to 20 minutes can give you that needed boost and energy to empower you to press through the next phase of your day.

Self-Care Task: Get a hair conditioning treatment or new hair style at the salon.

DAY 3: BUILD A LIFE OF CALMNESS

"I like the pause that tea allows." —Waris Ahluwalia

"Be still, and know that I am God. I will be exalted among the nations, I will be exalted in the earth!" (Psalm 46:10).

Be still.
Stop.
Refrain from moving.
Relax and withdraw.
Simply be quiet.

For many of us, these commands can cause us to feel unproductive, irresponsible, and weak. You are probably hearing that faint voice from your past saying, "An idle mind is the devil's workshop!"

On the contrary, in Psalm 46:10 we learn that God can speak to a mind that has made room for quiet and contemplation. He can reveal some of His deepest truths and treasures about Himself.

The harried and hurried life that presses in on us competes for mind space. Our minds are constantly moving at warp speed. We are too distracted by the cares of life. And our relationship stressors have us pulled from the inside out.

Being still is a command. It has benefits. We need to get to know and hear from God, our Master Creative Designer. He is constantly speaking, thinking of us and wants to do remarkably good things for us.

He loves hearing our voices and wants to whisper sweetness in our ears that reaches our hearts. He wants us to stand still and REST long enough to gaze upon His beauty and power because He knows that kind of experience with Him can deeply change us.

He is so intimately acquainted with us that every hair on our heads is numbered.

Why won't you . . .

Be still?

Stop?

Refrain from moving?

Relax and withdraw?

Simply be quiet?

Could it be that we don't know Him or trust Him? To know Him means you can distinguish His voice and ways from all others. It means that you have experienced His loving grace that is wider than the ocean. This truth became very real to me during my trip to Africa, with my husband. While viewing the Atlantic Ocean from the shores of Ghana, I saw the ocean's beauty and vastness which appeared endless. It's mind blowing and hard to fathom how wide and deep it is! The vastness of His love, likewise, is incomprehensive. It's deep!

Trusting Him means that you have tasted and seen that He is good. It means that you know beyond a shadow of doubt that He is The Great I AM, a truly present help in the time of trouble. The mere knowledge of His presence calms your anxious heart.

Our knowledge of who God is and what He can do in our lives brings us to a place of . . . being still.

This lifestyle is an act of obedience, one that must be cultivated. This silence is in the presence of a Master Creative Designer who is revealing Himself as He designs a Remarkable Life for your good and His glory.

What will it take for you to be still and get to know God? He is The Great I AM. He is all that you need. Find that right time and place for you to steep a cup of tea, sip and be still in His presence. Savor His goodness.

For me, this is one of my favorite grace and ease morning routines. By meditating-breathing spiritually, and practicing mindfulness, I command my inner Remarkable Woman to be still so that I can recognize God's powerful presence and experience Him throughout the day. This helps me practice being present in my rest and equips me to better manage my anxiety, depression and ADD.

Reflect and **Release Every Situation Totally**

1. Does the idea of being still seem hard to you? Why? Why not?
2. What is the right time and place for you to be still?
3. What sort of stillness routine could you create?

Tea Time and Conversation with God

Lord, I know that peace and stillness are your will for me, and yet I so often struggle to be still. I think that if I always hurry, I can create a great life for myself. Help me to see the incredible value of stillness. Help me learn to stop, rest and relax. Help me to trust You enough to stop working so hard. In Jesus' name, Amen.

Activate and Restfully Make It Happen

"The quieter you become, the more you can hear."
—*Ram Dass*

Contemplate what stillness looks like.

Create a place away from distraction to be still.

Celebrate the moments of knowingness. Practice a form of meditation which I call "spiritual breathing." Set your timer for seven minutes. Start by calmly and slowly inhaling to the count of seven which represents the number of completion. Imagine that the air is traveling from the soles of your feet to the crown of your head. Rest and feel it.

Hold it for a count of 11, imagining that God's Spirit is filling and embodying every cell and fiber of your being to empower you. Since the number 11 represents the number for chaos and disruption, intentionally and firmly push it out of you to the count of seven, which symbolizes completion. Repeat until your timer goes off.

Self-Care Task: Stare at the clouds. This was one of my favorite past times with my children during my days as a home-schooling mom, inspired by the children's book, *It Looked Like Spilt Milk.* Freely embrace your inner little Remarkable Woman. Use your imagination to describe what you see based on the shapes of the clouds. Relax and be still.

Day 4: Build a Life of Strength

"A woman is like a tea bag—you can't tell how strong she is until you put her in hot water." —Eleanor Roosevelt

"Have you not known? Have you not heard? The Lord is the everlasting God, the Creator of the ends of the earth. He does not faint or grow weary; his understanding is unsearchable. He gives power to the faint, and to him who has no might he increases strength. Even youths shall faint and be weary, and young men shall fall exhausted; but they who wait for the Lord shall renew their strength; they shall mount up with wings like eagles; they shall run and not be weary; they shall walk and not faint" (Isaiah 40:28-31 ESV).

Often, God allows difficult situations and adversities in our life that render us powerless. Wait for the LORD.

Feeling like giving up?

Pushed beyond your breaking point?

Wait for the LORD!

Lacking the courage needed to face your opposer?

Grappling with recovery from a loved one's or your own mental illness?

Rebuilding your life after a devastating personal or natural disaster?

Wait for the LORD!

Life is full of rough places that feel like a mountain too tough to climb. Many of us are tired and worn out spiritually, emotionally, and physically from serving and working. We feel powerless, overwhelmed, and hopeless. Hope in God will give you the strength and courage to rise above it all and soar. REST empowers you to renew your strength.

Your situation doesn't have to destroy or deter you from living your BEST Remarkable Life, every day. You are stronger than you know! God knows it very well. He is intimately acquainted with you. He has designed you for an abundant life. We must patiently wait on Him. As the Master Creative Designer, He is creating something remarkably beautiful out of our lives.

He sees and knows that we are weak, even if we appear to be strong. He is the everlasting God, who is always at work in us no matter how long it takes. He is supreme and sovereign over it all. And He wants us to be remarkable even through the struggle.

REST so that you can hear, see, and know.

Remarkable Women are like eagles. They know that resting and waiting on God helps you maintain your power and strength. They refuse to seek after a comfortable and crowded life. They know that protection can be found in solitude as while soaring above the rocky places in life that feel insurmountable.

Being alone teaches you to hear His voice. With keen vision, Remarkable Women have the courage to see beyond their limits and breaking points.

You can SOAR effortlessly. You don't have look like the struggle you are facing.

Be remarkably fearless.

Refuse to lose sight of your vision. REST. Only when we learn to REST in God will we have the wind of His Spirit that gives us the energy and power to soar with grace and ease, over our setbacks, challenges, and circumstances.

Need strength? Wait for the LORD!

Reflect and **Release Every Situation Totally**

1. When you are faced with a "rocky-like" circumstance or situation, do you tend to move toward rest or worry?
2. What does it look like to wait for the LORD?
3. How can you get to a place of rest when you're surrounded by chaos, conflict, and confusion?

Tea Time and Conversation with God

Lord, thank You that You are powerful and in control of all things. I know that with You on my side, nothing can stand against me. With You supporting me, no challenge can overwhelm me. Please help me to rest in Your power. Help me trust You and find rest in You when the oceans are tossed and stormy. Give me strength. Teach me to wait on You. You will renew my strength. In Jesus' name, Amen.

Activate and Restfully Make It Happen

Don't tell God how big your storm is, tell your storm how big God is. —Author Unknown

In your journal, write the words "rest" and "mountain" next to each other. Under each, write all the words that you associate with them. Then, spend 10 minutes contemplating how even in the storm, God can give you refreshing rest.

Find time during the middle of your work day to take a five to ten- minute sustained rest break. Push back your chair, close down your computer and "rest your eyes".

Self-Care Task: Read a book wearing fuzzy, comfortable socks.

DAY 5: BUILD A LIFE OF RESTORATION

"If you are cold, tea will warm you; if you are too heated, it will cool you; if you are depressed, it will cheer you; if you are excited, it will calm you."
—William Edward Gladstone

"For I will satisfy the weary soul, and every languishing soul I will replenish" (Jeremiah 31:25 ESV).

The life God has designed for us is intended to be remarkable. Yet too often, this chaotic and crazy broken world can bring misery instead.

Are you tired from trying to build a life of purpose and meaning?

Are you fainthearted from working yourself to the point of fatigue to provide for yourself and your family? Yet, seemingly you still do not have enough resources to make ends meet.

Have the troubles of life caused your soul to become weary and brokenhearted?

Are you working so hard to sustain and provide that you cannot enjoy the life you are creating?

Have hardships like destruction of your home, loss of a loved one, or chronic and debilitating illness invaded your life causing you sorrow?

Perhaps you find yourself in a difficult and desperate place. You are worn out and wondering why you should go on. I have experienced circumstances in seasons where it was all too much to bear.

I was someone who, before learning to rest deliberately, struggled with suicidal thoughts. Oftentimes I felt that perhaps it would be easier if I were to take myself out of my misery.

The drain on your soul can leave you feeling that life will never be remarkable—abundant and overflowing.

I'm so grateful that I learned you don't have to go it alone. Help is near.

As you learn to scale back, to slow life down to REST in Him, He will restore, replenish, and renew you. He will bring healing to your soul.

REST.

He loves you too much to allow you to serve on empty. He wants to fill you up to the point of overflow. He alone can satisfy your weary and wounded soul.

Deliberate REST is soul work. When we learn to scale back and slow down, we can connect deeply with the Remarkable God who abundantly renews and satisfies our empty and tired soul. He allows us to live a life of joy in His presence in the midst of sorrow, opposition, and misery, and make it a remarkable one filled with hope and peace. We can live The Life now.

The languishing soul is one that is faint, tired, and weary. But God promises to fill that same soul with good when we look to Him alone.

Reflect and Release Every Situation Totally

1. What circumstances are most draining to you?
2. What promises of God can give you rest in the midst of those circumstances?
3. What is it like to scale back, slow down, and connect deeply with God?

Tea Time and Conversation with God

Lord, thank You that You know every hair on my head and take a keen interest in all the details of my life. My struggles and trials are no secret to You, and I know You want to give me rest in the midst of them. Please teach me to draw near to You even in the midst of hardship. Help me to find the peace that surpasses understanding. In Jesus' name, Amen.

Activate and Restfully Make It Happen

"Restoration brings refreshment." —Lailah Gifty

Is there an area of your life where you feel drained and are in need of restoration? Write down five activities that are deeply restful for you. Don't feel guilty about indulging in this. Your goal is to build a life of restoration by design.

Remember, God wants you to rest so that you are experiencing an abundant life from a place of wholeness. Once you've identified your restful activities, use your Rest and Build planner to fit them into your schedule each week this month. Great things can happen when you do.

Self-Care Task: Learn to say "No." It's a complete sentence. Remember that practice make permanent. Practice saying No!

DAY 6: BUILD A LIFE OF PEACE

*One sip of this will bathe the drooping spirits in
delight, beyond the bliss of dreams.* —John Milton

*"In peace I will both lie down and sleep; for You alone, O
Lord, make me dwell in safety"* (Psalm 4:8).

We were created to live a life of security and peace. Security is one of my utmost core values. It gives me peace of mind.

Of course, in a fallen world there are many things that attack our security:

Pain, persecution, and pressure

Fear for yourself and your family

Disappointment and guilt over your own sins or shortcomings

Betrayal from someone that you have ministered to who is attacking your character

When people shame you and speak unkind, evil, and untrue things about you

In these periods of trial and difficulty, learn to rest.

How? Regardless of the taunts and attacks, the Lord will protect us. No one can hurt or harm you without God's permission. Because of God's sovereignty and love for us, we can experience peace. Suffering doesn't have to disturb our sleep.

Close your weary eyes by keeping your focus on the God who never sleeps. He is there to watch over us. Dwell. Rest in Him. Lie down and sleep well.

His love for us is eternal and unconditional.

We don't have to try to take matters into our hands. Our sovereign God is in control.

Confessing your sins and experiencing His forgiveness gives you peace. Sin will rob you of your sleep. Repent and choose to walk in a different, new path today. God will help you if you open yourself to His truth.

Allow His joy and peace to override your anxiety. Turn your worries, doubts, and fears over to Him.

Continue to live a life worth the remark for His glory by trusting Him.

Pray for those who are against you. Put your life in the hands of the Master Creative Designer and REST well.

He has the power to keep us safe. He is reliable and trustworthy.

This is a great reminder before bedtime! Lie down and sleep well tonight.

Reflect and Release Every Situation Totally

1. How does knowing that God doesn't sleep allow you to trust Him more?
2. What worries and fears keep you from getting enough sleep?
3. What would a peaceful, God-honoring nighttime routine look like?

Tea Time and Conversation with God

Lord, I know that sleep is a gift from You. Forgive me for all the times I've neglected it. Help me to take full advantage of Your wonderful gift of sleep. Help me sleep without anxiety or stress. Help me trust You when I lay down to rest. I know that You hold all things in your hands, which means I can sleep soundly in peace. In Jesus' name, Amen.

Activate by Restfully Making It Happen

If God be our God, He will give us peace in trouble. When there is a storm without, He will make peace within. The world can create trouble in peace, but God can create peace in trouble. —Thomas Watson

Write out your current nightly routine. Does it help you to sleep peacefully or does it make you more stressed? Personally, I love putting body cream on my feet, putting on my fuzzy socks, and climbing into bed. It not only relaxes my tired feet but softens and repairs the skin. Write down a new routine that would lend to a peaceful, restful night. Make sure to schedule it in your Rest and Build Planner.

Self-Care Task: Create an evening routine that helps restfully prepare for the upcoming day. Keep your items, like the ones from your Sabbath day basket from Day 1, accessible so that you are more likely to practice it consistently.

DAY 7: BUILD A LIFE OF PROTECTION

Today I'd like to sit and sip,
Forget about the world a bit,
Ignore the things I have to do,
And just enjoy a cup or two.
—Author Unknown

"He who dwells in the shelter of the Most High will abide in the shadow of the Almighty" (Psalm 91:1 NASB).

Shelter is a basic human need. We can't possibly survive the elements of the seasons of life without proper shelter. God, the Most High, loves and cares for us.

The shelter He provides protects our well-being. The elements of the seasons of life, adversity, burnout, barrenness, and emotional storms can cause fatigue and weakness. Resting in His shelter gives us the strength to continue the journey of pursuing the Remarkable Life.

Are you seeking a place to put your valuables to keep them from getting into the wrong hands? Our God, the highest ruler over everything, is the perfect source of safety and refuge. He is not hiding from us. He is the place where we can hide and find safety and rest in Him.

King David found comfort during a time of betrayal from his one-time friend, King Saul.

Betrayal can destroy what seemed a perfect future, dissolve your priorities, and remain constantly just below your conscious thoughts for a very long time . . . especially when it comes from people that you have loved the most. It can take you to a place where your highest goals are gone and there is nothing left. In the pain and demoralization that betrayal brings, you can lose sight of the beauty of the Remarkable Life.

But with God, El Elyon, The Most High God, beauty can come out of dark places! His presence brings comfort for your worries, stress, and problems. He is a welcome retreat from persecution. Through it all, He will, as I constantly remind myself, "bring beauty into being". Rest. Remain in the shadow of the Almighty, the all-sufficient God. His presence gives peace, His hands offer hope and His mind offers a way out.

Being in His shadow brings closeness, connectedness, and intimacy. Rest in Him. If you know Him personally, through His Son, you will find Him. Jesus is near. Just as the shadow can't be found without the sun, we can't find God without the Son, the Light of the world. If you don't know how, God has created the perfect plan by trusting His Son Jesus to be your loving Savior. He wants to connect with you. According to Rev. 3:20, when you invite Him into your life, without hesitation, He comes in.

Let Him protect you from hurt, harm, and damage imposed by those who betray you and seek to destroy your reputation. Look for His shadow and REST.

Reflect and Release Every Situation Totally

1. What does it mean to you that God is YOUR shelter?
2. When things get tough, do you instinctively run to God for shelter? If not, why not?

3. What are some simple, practical ways to take shelter in God?

Tea Time and Conversation with God

Lord, I praise that You are my shelter and my hiding place. When I'm sheltered by You, I am safe and at peace. You are my protector, my refuge, my rock, and my shield. Teach me to run to You in times of strife and heartache and stress. Teach me to find my shelter under your protective wings. In Jesus' name, Amen.

Activate and Restfully Make Things Happen

"What matters most is how well you walk through the fire." —Charles Bukowski

In your journal, write down *all* the words you associate with "shelter". Now write full sentences in which you detail how God is that for you. For example, "God is my shelter. God is my shield. He always protects me. He guards me from the attacks of the enemy. Nothing can get through this shelter."

In your home, create your hiding space symbolic of a shelter and a desired safe haven. Express your creativity by fixing it up so that it draws you in and satisfies your need to be in His presence. Perhaps add your essential oils, diffuser, teapot and teacup, candles in your favorite "power" color or scent, pillows, a basket with Sabbath day and self-care items, etc. Schedule a date and time in your planner to retreat to your special shelter and REST in God's presence.

Restful Sleep: Sleep is an Act of Faith

We are never more vulnerable than we are as we sleep. With our eyes shut and body still, many of our muscles are paralyzed (to prevent us from acting out our dreams). To sleep is to find rest in knowing that we are not in control, that a God who is far greater watches over us. *"In peace I will lie down and sleep, for You alone, LORD, make me dwell in safety,"* (Psalm 4:8).

If we trust in ourselves, we will know a sleep that is fitful, fretful, and restless. In contrast, when we go to sleep as an act of faith, entrusting ourselves to God's keeping, then we will enjoy the peaceful, restful sleep that God provides. *"I lie down and sleep; I wake again, because the Lord sustains me,"* (Psalm 3:5).

By faith, sleep well and activate your best life.

Self-Care Task: Create a daily Tea Time ritual— Drink a hot cup of tea at the same time each day or at least daily.

Day 8: Build a Life of Dependence

*When tea becomes ritual, it takes its place at the
heart of our ability to see greatness in small things.
Where is beauty to be found? In great things that, like
everything else, are doomed to die, or in small things
that aspire to nothing, yet know how to set a jewel of
infinity in a single moment?* —Muriel Barbery

*"The Lord is my shepherd; I shall not want. He makes me lie
down in green pastures. He leads me beside still waters. He
restores my soul"* (Psalm 23:1-3 ESV).

The life of a shepherd is one of protection, provision, and persistence. They spend every waking moment caring for the sheep. Under their watchful eye, they keep them out of harm's way from wolves, jackals, lions, and thieves. And without hesitation, they are willing to lay down their lives for the sheep out of love.

Shepherds guide their sheep to a place to drink where they can drink with peace. Sheep are feeble minded, helpless, and next to impossible to train. They are easily frightened by moving water, which makes it difficult for them to drink.

Like sheep need someone to lead them, we need the Lord to be our shepherd as we journey in life. We are prone to wander and get hopelessly lost and off our course. Life was meant to be remarkable—overflowing and full of meaning. We must listen for His voice—the voice of the Shepherd. We can't afford to *not* live life without Him. We are completely dependent on Him to find true soul rest as we allow Him to guide, nurture, protect, and provide for us.

We are to keep our eyes on Him so that we don't get lost, depleted, or injured. We need to rest in Him and allow Him to carry us when the issues of life wear us down. Every need we have, He is more than capable of supplying. He wants the best for us. And He knows what will happen if we continue to try to guide ourselves through life. God wants to give you a place to slow down where you experience peace and rest. If you lack wisdom about where to rest, the Good Shepherd will guide you.

Reflect and Release Every Situation Totally

1. What are the specific ways a shepherd cares for the sheep?
2. Why do you need to depend on the Good Shepherd?
3. How does God shepherd you?

Tea Time and Conversation with God:

Lord, thank You that You are my shepherd, the one who leads me to still waters and green pastures. Thank You that You watch over me, guide me, and keep me on the right path. Thank You that when I wander away, You shepherd me back. Teach me to have great confidence in your shepherding. In Jesus' name, Amen.

Activate by Restfully Making Things Happen

If God sends us on strong paths, we are provided strong shoes. —Corrie Ten Boom

Go for a nature walk. As you walk, look around and ponder how God cares for and shepherds everything in creation. He provides for the birds. He showers rain on the flowers. These things don't worry; instead, they trust their shepherd to provide. Pray that God would teach you to trust Him in the same way. Complete dependence on Him gives rest that makes life worth living.

Self-Care Task: Take photos of something in nature that makes you smile. Compile them in a virtual look-book. Look at it often for inspiration.

DAY 9: BUILD A WORRY-FREE LIFE

Tea purifies spirit, removes anxiety and nervousness, brings ease and comfort, and is conducive to meditation. —Author Unknown

"Do not be anxious about anything, but in everything by prayer and supplication with thanksgiving let your requests be made known to God. And the peace of God, which surpasses all understanding, will guard your hearts and your minds in Christ Jesus" (Philippians 4:6-7 ESV).

E veryone is prone to feel a little anxious every now and then. It's a normal human emotion. But there are those of us who are prone to fear, anxiety, and worry on a much deeper level.

These people, myself included, worry over the things that *have* happened, and those that happened only in their mind but *feel* real. Every symptom in their body is the signal of a chronic illness. Acute self-consciousness, phobias, irritability, sleep deprivation, panic attacks, and feeling uneasy in social settings all leave them exhausted.

Fears of not measuring up, or not being good enough, trigger feelings of anxiety. For those watching and attempting to be a support, it can be baffling as they wonder:

"How can you possibly lose sight of reality when you have so much going for you?"

"Why can't you just live in the moment?"

"You just need to take one day at a time."

"Don't worry about the future; it hasn't happened yet."

It's all well-meaning advice. But there's more to it than just that. Globally, more than 300 million people suffer from depression, and 260 million suffer from anxiety disorders—many live with both conditions. A study by the World Health Organization found that such disorders cost the global economy $1 trillion in lost productivity each year. It is a problem that is not going away and probably increasing.[3]

Worry and anxiety problems can be random and unpredictable. And the effects are devastating and life-altering. There's nothing worse than feeling as if you are going crazy while your loved ones are watching and feeling frustrated and helpless.

But just as these feelings and statistics are real, so is recovery.

The Apostle Paul gives one of the best solutions to this endless fretting: **A restful dependency on God.**

I want you to emotionally get honest—"naked and not ashamed." Think about what is making you anxious. Call it out and speak it by name. Often, things we keep in the dark also keep us in powerless places. Bring that anxiety and worry into the light so that God, the Father of Lights, can bring you healing.

Take the load off of yourself and throw it onto God. Invite God's calm into your life. Seek help from the Master Creative Designer. Trust Him to see you through it. Look for ways to express a heart of gratitude and thanksgiving back to Him. In return, by faith, and in action, commit yourself to stress less and experience His peace.

Reflect and Release Every Situation Totally

1. What things are currently making you anxious and worried?

2. Why are they causing you to worry?

3. How can you cast those worries on God right now?

Tea Time and Conversation with God

Lord, thank You that I can depend on You. I may not have all the answers, but You do. You give a peace that passes understanding. You give rest even in the midst of my deepest anxieties. Teach me to find all of my rest in You. Teach me to not lean on my own understanding. Teach me that even when I don't have all the answers, I can trust You. In Jesus' name, Amen.

Activate by Restfully Making Things Happen

Look around and you'll be distressed. Look within, and you'll be depressed. Look to the Lord, and you'll be at rest. —Corrie Ten Boom

Pour a cup of your favorite tea. In your journal, list out five things that are currently making you anxious. Write out the details of exactly why you're feeling anxious about these things. After you've identified your anxiety triggers, write out five affirmations, such as, "I am stronger than my fear" or "I AM a Remarkable Woman of peace" to help you push past your moments of anxiety. Then spend seven to ten minutes praying and handing these anxious things over to God.

Self-Care Task: Set your timer for 15 minutes and write uninhibited in your journal.

DAY 10: BUILD AN UNSHAKEABLE LIFE

A cup of tea would restore my normality.
—Douglas Adams

"Truly my soul finds rest in God; my salvation comes from him. Truly he is my rock and my salvation; he is my fortress, I will never be shaken" (Psalm 62:1–2).

We are constantly tempted to live a life of self-sufficiency. Our innate pride does not want help and wants to be able to accomplish *what* it wants *when* it wants.

God frequently appoints severe trials in our lives so we can learn experientially that we are not our own saviors. Everything we accomplish in our lives is merely due to the creative activity and personal blessing of God!

I have experienced situations where I could have been shaken to my core and had to rely on God. In living the Remarkable Life, He desires that we look to Him and His all-sufficient grace and goodness as the treasure of our lives and the hope of our souls. If we have any delusions about being our own savior (or, for that matter, lord), God has no problem in creating or allowing precisely the kind of circumstances that will usher us back to Him.

Because God is our Master Creative Designer and Savior, only He can be our sufficient source of rest. And it is only as we rest in Him will we find ourselves standing on a solid rock. Therefore as we are building our best Remarkable Life, nothing can shake us.

Reflect and **Release Every Situation Totally**

1. Has God brought any difficult circumstances into your life?
2. What good things is He trying to teach you through these circumstances?
3. What ways are you tempted to be self-sufficient?

Tea Time and Conversation with God

Lord, thank You that all my sufficiency is found in You. Please forgive me for all the times I've relied on my own strength and abilities rather than You. When life gets challenging, help me to run to You. When I find myself overwhelmed, help me find my strength in You. You are good and I trust You. In Jesus' name, Amen.

Activate by Restfully Making Things Happen

"In the time of darkest defeat, victory may be nearest."
—William McKinley

The essential oils found in aromatherapy can have an uplifting effect on your mind, spirit, and body. Light your favorite aromatherapy candle or diffuse your favorite oil and dim the lights. Simply sit and be still for seven to ten minutes. Every time a worry or fear tries to intrude on your peace, tempting you to be shaken, command it to flee. **R**elease **E**very **S**ituation **T**otally to God. Enjoy the simple rest that God allows you to have in the midst of building and living your life by design and not by default, with grace and ease.

Self-Care Task: Buy a new bath fizz bomb and add essential oils to your bath water. Take a hot aromatherapy soak. Relax and enjoy the fizzle.

DAY 11: BUILD A LIFE OF RETREATING

The most trying hours in life are between four o'clock and the evening meal. A cup of tea at this time adds a lot of comfort and happiness. —Royal S. Copeland

"Come with me by yourselves to a quiet place and get some rest" (Mark 6:31).

I n Mark 6:30–32, the apostles have just returned from a ministry journey the Lord had sent them on. Tasked with declaring to Israel that her Messiah had come, the apostles were anointed as His representatives with His power to authenticate His ministry and proclaim his power and character.

This likely would have been an exuberant, if not extremely exhausting, time of ministry! Our Lord had found Himself regularly mobbed by people who wanted a miracle, often for selfish reasons. Thus, He understood the emotional and mental tax of trying to meet the needs of so many people. As people come to Jesus, the Lord wisely invites them to come away with Him for a time of rest and refreshment.

In Mark verse 31, the renewal time the disciples experience is short-lived, as their location soon becomes the site for the feeding of the 5,000 (Mark 6:35–44). Still, note the Lord's wisdom: He recognizes, appreciates, and even affirms the humanity and frailty of His disciples and values them enjoying rest.

He understands that they need refreshment and a place to recharge. And likely wrestling with doubts, they also need to think through what they have just experienced and how they can maximize their usefulness to Him.

Do you realize the Lord has the same attentiveness and kindness toward you? That He is sensitive to the wounds and weariness you have received in service to Him? You, too, are one of His disciples. Answer His call and come away with Him to rest for a while, that you might emerge with great clarity and energy to serve Him with effectiveness and joy.

Reflect and Release Every Situation Totally

1. Do you believe that God wants you to have rest?
2. How often do you imitate Jesus and "get away" and rest for a while?
3. What keeps you from following the example of Jesus?

Tea Time and Conversation with God

Lord, thank You that You care about my rest. You want to bless me with the gift of rest, and for that, I'm so grateful. If You call me to rest, I know it must be a very good thing. Teach me to put things aside and get away to rest for a while. Teach me to lay aside the weights and cares that burden me and to find rest in my Savior. In Jesus' name, Amen.

Activate by Restfully Making Things Happen

If we seek solitary retreat, you will be more often refreshed. —Lailah Gifty

Are you tired, overwhelmed, and overworked? Are you in need of clarity about your life and what you have been called to build? Create a one-day solo retreat where you pull away and unplug for a time of deep contemplation, celebration, and creation. In solitude, practice mindfulness as you release every situation totally to Him to gain a fresh perspective. Use this as a time of reflection about your life, desired leadership brand, purpose, and impact. Set goals, plans, and activities to help you reach them. Celebrate all that God has allowed you to accomplish and experience. Dream and create ways to restfully activate your life by making a greater contribution to the world that adds lasting value.

Self-Care Task: Restfully wake up in the morning. Fight the urge to get up quickly. Practice getting up slowly without the sound of a blaring alarm clock. Allow yourself to be fully, awake and in the moment.

DAY 12: BUILD A LIFE OF CONTENTMENT

Tea is drunk to forget the dim of the world. —T'ien
Yi-heng

*"Be still before the LORD and wait patiently for him; fret
not yourself over the one who prospers in his way, over the
man who carries out evil devices!"* (Psalm 37:7 ESV).

D o you ever feel like you can do all of the right things, but
no matter what, things just don't seem to work out in your
favor? It's hard watching people who seem to enjoy the pain
they are causing on others find favor and fruitfulness. Most of us
can recognize injustice when we see it and it's hard to make sense of.

Also, the more you focus on people like this who prosper, by
looking at what they have, and how they accomplished it, the more
likely you are to get your life off course. Sometimes the truth is that
they fiercely want their goals or are more determined to go after the
life of their dreams, even if it's "by any means necessary."

Could it be that negativity, fear, and "stinking thinking" are
dragging you down and keeping you from living your best life?
While this reality stings, instead of allowing it to cause you to grieve
or burn with anger, choose to be still in God's presence. Allow Him
to hold you close and reassure you that He is in control.

Don't get discouraged or frustrated; reset and get connected
with God. Maintain your values; stand for what is right in His eyes.

Seek to align your thoughts with God's power to prevail and make that your focus.

Let's go back to the Garden of Eden where it all began. Because of the first sin, we live in a fallen and broken world. This means pain and brokenness are a reality of life for now. Proper commitment and consecration to the Lord will enable you to rise above adversity and know His peace and blessing, even through your tears.

Nice things, whether they be clothes, cars, houses, trinkets that we gather, riches that we accumulate, land that we purchase, or trophies we are awarded, are all temporary!

Things received here are not always a sign of God's favor. They may bring comfort but it is temporary. Deliberately REST in Him and continue to build the life to which you have been called making your focus on the eternal not the temporal.

Reflect and Release Every Situation Totally

1. What negative thoughts and fears are threatening your contentment?
2. How can you get connected to God and replace those fears with faith?
3. What actions can you take to align your focus with God's plans and timing for you?

Tea Time and Conversation with God

Lord, forgive me for all the times I've focused on my fears and negative thoughts instead of Your power and goodness that is working on my behalf. Help me to find my rest, peace, and blessing in You. Protect me from the discouraging thoughts and fears that the enemy wants me to believe. Teach

me to put all my focus on You. Help me to find my content-
ment in You. In Jesus' name, Amen.

Activate by Restfully Making Things Happen

If you don't stick to your values when they're being
tested, they're not values: they're hobbies. —Jon
Stewart

Relaxation techniques help to put your mind, body, and spirit in a restful place. Here's one that I find helpful: bring your body to a resting position. Turn on relaxation music, like waterfalls (I love listening to my recording of the sound of roaring waves of the Atlantic Ocean off the shores of Ghana) or sit in silence. Slowly count to seven while bringing your shoulders up to your ears, hold for 11 seconds, then count to seven while lowering your shoulders. Do three sets. Then, rotate your shoulders forward seven times, then backward. Finish by rotating one shoulder at a time, forward and backward, seven times.

Self-Care Task: Be spontaneous. Do something on the spur of the moment! Take a drive, buy flowers for yourself, visit a pet store and play with the puppies or kittens, go to lunch with a friend, or look up something inspiring or at least funny on the Internet!

DAY 13: BUILD A LIFE OF HOPE

One sip of this will bathe the drooping spirits in delight, beyond the bliss of dreams. John Milton

"And to you who are troubled rest with us, when the Lord Jesus shall be revealed from heaven with his mighty angels" (2 Thessalonian 1:7 KJV).

The believer's hope is the return of our Lord. On that glorious day, He will renew our bodies and begin His rule upon this earth. The believers to whom Paul wrote were the recipients of much persecution and trial by the unbelieving world around them. Yet they manifested a remarkable, fearless commitment to the Lord and His ways.

Isn't it something that we are promised rest when the Lord returns? Rest from our trials. Rest from pain. Rest from persecution, from sickness, from suffering, from discomfort, from loneliness, from confusion—from all the things that make this a broken, fallen world.

If you are suffering, draw your thinking and affections to the promised hope of rest, eternally, and relief at the return of Christ. He loves you and has good things planned for you in this life and the next as you remain faithful to Him. In the meantime, hang in there and continue to release every situation totally to Him. The best **REST** is yet to come!

Reflect and **Release** **Every** **Situation** **Totally**

1. How does the return of Christ encourage you now?
2. How does the return of Christ give you strength to keep going now?
3. What ways can you rest today with an expectancy of the coming future in mind?

Tea Time and Conversation with God

Lord, I'm grateful that this world isn't my final home. I'm so thankful that a day is coming when You will return and all that's wrong with the world will be made right. Help me to actively look forward to that day. Help me to find hope in that day. Help me to live in light of that day. In Jesus' name, Amen.

Activate by Restfully Making Things Happen

The best thing about the future is that it comes only one day at a time. —Abraham Lincoln

To rejuvenate and restore ourselves mentally and physically, we must learn to rest. Take an assessment to evaluate the times of day you tend to feel sluggish or fatigued. It is not uncommon to experience brain drain midday. Be mindful of the projects you take on during those times. Whatever that time of the day, don't fight it. Listen to your body and rest it. Intentionally, schedule a 15-20 minute rest break where you can rest your mind and body. Try to make this rest break a daily habit.

Self-Care Task: Get Moving! Exercise for at least 30 minutes. Create excitement in your workout. Try something new and let it be fun.

DAY 14: BUILD A LIFE OF UNCONDITIONAL LOVE

The spirit of the tea beverage is one of peace, comfort, and refinement. —Arthur Gray

"The LORD appeared to us in the past, saying: 'I have loved you with an everlasting love;" (Jeremiah 31:3).

Jeremiah, the weeping prophet, declared a truth that is timeless: God's love for us knows no bounds. His love for us is eternal. In Hebrew, this kind of love is called *hesed*. It is the covenantal, unfailing, ever-present love needed for the journey. I love how one translation describes it: "With the old love I have loved thee."

Now *that* is a forever kind of love! The Jewish people experienced persecution and wandering in the wilderness before entering the promised land. Needless to say, their shortcomings and failures made it easy for them to feel that they didn't matter to God. Yet, God wanted them to know that He had a single-hearted devotion to them no matter what. They could rest knowing that they were loved unconditionally.

Likewise, regardless of what you are faced with on this journey to restfully building and experiencing the Remarkable Life, you must not forget that you matter to God. As a Remarkable Woman of God, stay on the journey and remember that you are valuable in

His eyes! He loves you deeply and unconditionally. So make it your priority to REST.

Trust God to provide for you completely. No matter what your circumstances look like right now. We waste too much time worrying about things that are out of our control.

Rest is that place where you replace worry with worship. Resting in Him allows us to improve the quality of our lives. From personal experience, I have learned that rest will keep us from stress, the cause of so many devastating health issues and the burnout that threatens us.

Reflect and Release Every Situation Totally

1. Have you experienced the Lord's personal love for you?
2. How can knowing the Lord has loved you with a loyal, everlasting sort of love encourage you in the difficulties and trials you face in a fallen world?
3. Do you believe the Lord loves you personally, or do you still doubt Him?

Tea Time and Conversation with God

Lord God, thank You that because of Christ I am perfectly loved by You. Please help me to receive, believe, and rest in Your love for me regardless of how I feel or the lies my flesh and the devil tell me. Please transform me by Your love, that I would be a sparkling testimony of Your beauty and sufficiency. Glorify Yourself through my life. In Jesus' name, Amen.

Activate by Restfully Making Things Happen

Thou hast made us for thyself, O Lord, and our heart is restless until it finds its rest in thee. —Augustine of Hippo, *Confessions*

Get a massage. There's nothing more relaxing than an hour on the table in the hands of a professional massage therapist. Studies have shown repeatedly that a rubdown washes away worries while increasing serotonin, dopamine, and the hormones that make you feel happy and relaxed. Grab your planner and schedule a massage this month.

Restful Sleep: Sleep is a Brain Cleaner

In addition to being a necessity for physical health, sleep is essential for the mind and helps regulate your mood.[4] While insufficient sleep and sleep problems are linked to depression and anxiety, healthy sleep promotes learning, memory consolidation, positive mood, and creativity.

The idea that the brain is inactive during sleep is a major misconception. Behind the curtain of sleep, the brain processes the information gathered during the day and makes preparations for the day to follow. For example, recent research suggests that toxins and waste products that build up in the brain during wakefulness are "flushed out" of the brain during sleep, as cerebrospinal fluid is pumped into and out of the brain at a more rapid pace.[5]

Another recent study confirmed that synapses, which are the connections between neurons in the brain, are "scaled back" or "pruned" during sleep, preventing the brain from becoming overloaded.[6] Given these critical functions of sleep, it is no wonder that sleep problems may be an early sign of dementia and Alzheimer's disease.[7]

Self-Care Task: Take a scenic drive. Enjoy God's creation. Roll down the windows and smell and feel the air. Allow it to remind you that God's unconditional love is surrounding you.

DAY 15: BUILD A RENEWED LIFE

Tea is a cup of life. —Author Unknown

"Therefore if anyone is in Christ, he is a new creature; the old things passed away; behold, new things have come" (2 Corinthians 5:17 NASB).

Growing up I struggled to see my value and significance. Many times I either felt that I was unlovable or unloving. I simply desired to love and be loved. I mistakenly thought that I had found that kind of love during my senior year of college. But after a painful breakup, I was in need of a healing for my broken heart. At my mom's suggestion, I agreed to go to church with her with renewed hopes. Perhaps the pastor could pray for the healing and restoration of our relationship. I wanted Randy back!

But, thankfully, God had other plans. Making my way to the altar at the end of the service, I never expected to be introduced to the lover of my soul. After experiencing God's unconditional love and Jesus' desire to renew my soul and provide with an overflowing life I surrendered my life to Him.

To know Christ is to know Him as the one who delivers and rescues us from a life of darkness and despair. We were created to live a Remarkable Life! And when we come to know Him personally and allow Him to take residence in our hearts, we experience a spiritual regeneration. Our souls are renewed and able to connect with God.

We also experience the ability to go within ourselves in a way that had not existed before. When we allow His presence in our lives, we have the freedom to see the world with a new heart and new eyes. God reinvents us so that we have the desire to live a life of obedience to His purpose and plan, in order to position ourselves to carry out "good works" that put Him on display.

You can draw near to our Heavenly Father through prayer. As you run to Him, He will embrace you in the arms of love! Jeremiah 29:12 states, *"Then you will call upon me and come and pray to me, and I will hear you."*

I have never regretted calling on Him over thirty-seven years ago, during my time of despair. Not only did I receive a new heart and a new life but a new identity. I have been chosen—purposefully reinvented, to be The Remarkable Woman destined to live a life worth noticing and that matters for His name sake.

Remember when you pray, God hears you. If you have not done so, take a moment now to write a prayer to God expressing your desire to renew and reinvent your life from the inside out so that you too can live and lead like The Remarkable Woman of God.

Reflect and Release Every Situation Totally

1. Have you had any past experiences with God or faith that have shaped your life?
2. When you think of God "renewing and reinventing your life", what does that mean to you?
3. Do you think you've experience the "renewal" I talk about?

Note: If not, please don't hesitate to reach out to me.

Tea Time and Conversation with God

Lord God, thank You so much for the glorious gift of salvation. I am forever in awe that You would extend mercy to me because of Christ. Please help me to continue to trust You, believing You are better than the lies of sin and Satan. Please make my life a pure testimony of Your saving grace that all the glory might go to You. In Jesus' name, Amen.

Activate by Restfully Making Things Happen

Knowing that we are fulfilling God's purpose is the only thing that gives rest to the restless human heart.
—Chuck Colson

Go for a short walk outside and look at all the life that is bursting around you. The trees, the sun, the sky, birds, insects—there is life everywhere. Now consider the beauty of having God come into your heart and give you HIS life. Isn't that remarkably good news? They, like you, were created with a purpose in mind. Journal your thoughts.

Speaking of purpose, God, our Master Creative Designer, designs with a purpose and flair. He creates nothing by accident. Just as businesses were started to solve a problem, so were we. Our purpose in life is to solve a specific problem. This is commonly known as your 'why' or life purpose. To discover it requires that you look inward and begin to access the story of your life, the value of your presence, the reason you wake up every morning and the desired impact you want to make on the world. Lastly, your purpose is usually connected with a pain that by God's grace you have overcome or are overcoming. And, in turn, you feel called to take a stand for others who are in need of support and encouragement in the same area.

Self-Care Task: Look at your childhood pictures and create a timeline of your life. Celebrate your wins.

DAY 16: BUILD A LIFE OF REFRESHMENT

This morning's tea makes yesterday distant. —Author Unknown

"It is in vain that you rise up early and go late to rest, eating the bread of anxious toil; for he gives to his beloved sleep" (Psalm 127:2 ESV).

The issue is not if you are an early morning riser, a night owl, or a workaholic. Instead, it's about your willingness to depend on God. Waking up early and going to bed late doesn't make us more successful in life . . . nor does worry. And the latter only makes it difficult for us to rest.

God has the power to cause us to rest! In the midst of a busy and hurried life, we can experience tranquility. A Remarkable Life is one in which you can experience rest without anxious toil. We are His Beloved! Being known as His beloved is a reminder of His favor upon your life. A life of dependency on Him will create the freedom to serve Him with endurance and joy. Refuse to allow the affairs of life to drain you and sap your energy to the point of exhaustion. Rest.

We tend to work feverishly, like we are running out of time. It weighs our hearts down. The Remarkable Life that we are seeking to build must be built by God. We forget that when sin entered the picture that we were doomed to work by the sweat of our brows, consumed with anxiety over how our needs would be provided.

We are living off of fumes. A lack of sleep hinders us from executing with excellence. God cares about us and everything that is happening in our lives. We need more sleep. Too often we are so worried that we can't rest. On the job we are working to the point of exhaustion for a promotion that seems elusive and almost impossible. We may have a spouse who constantly causes us to question our value and beauty, so we work to prove that we are desirable. Maybe our business doesn't seem to be growing in spite of our best efforts.

To rest doesn't mean that you are being idle or lazy. Nor does it mean to do nothing but live a life of leisure. As we seek to build a Remarkable Life where we are branded and marked as Remarkable Women, we know the benefit of intentionally inviting rest into our lives. We must learn to quiet ourselves down and find refreshment in being in the moment.

I spent so many years feeling like I was burning the candle at both ends—going to bed late and getting up early with very little to sustain me through the day. As I have learned to refocus my thinking, pursue the Lord's power, and trust Him alone to meet my needs I can experience the refreshment He brings through rest. You can, too, as you look to Him alone.

Reflect and Release Every Situation Totally

What areas of your life show you struggle to believe everything does not depend on you, and that you are not trusting in the Lord to provide for you?

1. If you are overworked and over-committed, why do you think that is? Could it be because you feel your worth and value are tied to what you do, rather than who you are because of Christ?

2. What are the choices you can make that will demonstrate faith in God's sufficiency and personal care, as opposed to believing you are self-sufficient?

3. What simple things in life bring refreshment to your soul?

Tea Time and Conversation with God:

Heavenly Father, I confess that I worry and try to do too much! Please forgive me for hustling and grinding instead of resting in Your sufficiency and provision. Please forgive me for trying to be my own savior instead of resting in all You have done (and will do) for me. Help me to look to You alone instead of trying to prove myself through what I do. Help me to believe I am perfectly accepted in Christ and that all I do must flow out of that perfect acceptance. In Jesus' name, Amen.

Activate by Restfully Making It Happen

Rest is not idleness, and to lie sometimes on the grass under trees on a summer's day, listening to the murmur of the water, or watching the clouds float across the sky, is by no means a waste of time. —John Lubbock

Get away from your hyper-connected, overstimulated life and find rest by indulging in water therapy. Whether it's a pool, spa, a lake at the park, or the ocean, in solitude, escape to this refreshing place. Enjoy the sights, sounds, and smells allowing it to soothe and bring comfort to your soul. Find scriptures that deal with being refreshed. Record your observations and thoughts about the verses and this experience in your journal.

_____  _____

Self-Care Task: Draw yourself a warm bath with lavender bath salts and spend some time praying and asking God to help you build your Remarkable Life from a place of rest in Him.

_____

DAY 17: BUILD A LIFE OF BEAUTY

"Tea is like a beautiful woman, never to be judged for her appearance. She has to be judged by her character." —Sethia

"Rather, it should be that of your inner self, the unfading beauty of a gentle and quiet spirit, which is of great worth in God's sight" (1 Peter 3:4).

Remember the well-known classic fairy tale, *Sleeping Beauty? The beautiful princess, Aurora, who was cursed and falls under a deep sleep. The only thing that can awaken her is a kiss from a prince.* For many of us, if you were caught sleeping too much, you were ridiculed and called Sleeping Beauty! Leaving you to feel that sleep was a curse instead of a blessing and gift. There is a connection between beauty and rest. Sleep is a wonderful beauty regimen. And, as we are learning, sleep is essential for us to protect our true beauty, from the inside out, as Remarkable Women. This extended rest gives us the ability to think clearly, be refreshed, and respond to others more graciously.

The true beauty that we are seeking to build begins on the inside. It must begin with our character and attitude. Having a gentle and quiet spirit is oftentimes seen as a negative or curse. We tend to see it as a sign of weakness or being a doormat.

It is deeper than keeping your mouth closed. On the contrary, it means you have a truly still and rested spirit that knows the beauty of resting in the presence of your heavenly prince. He gives you peace and lavishes His kisses upon your life in the form of blessings. You then from a place of overflow are known for "bringing beauty into being" because of the way your presence invites calm and peace into a situation. Your true beauty is also marked by an unhurried life even when confronted with the issues and stressors of life.

How can you experience this kind of beauty? Come to Christ. Look to Him as your sufficiency and example. As you look to Him by faith, you will know His power and sustaining grace, and He will transform you into a remarkably beautiful woman who "brings beauty into being."

Reflect and Release Every Situation Totally:

1. Are you consciously looking to Christ to be your sufficiency and rest, or are you trying to do things on your own power?

2. How are you seeking to learn from Christ as His disciple? Learning from Him is tied to experiencing His rest.

3. Will you trust the Lord to give you His strength as you trust Him, or do you doubt His ability or willingness?

Tea Time and Conversation with God:

Lord Jesus, thank You so much that You promise me rest as I trust and learn from You. Please give me a teachable spirit to hear what You say through Your Word and to do what it says. Please give me a willingness to see my true beauty from the inside out and trust You to take care of me and do what is best for me even if I cannot understand what You are doing. Thank You for the hope You have given me because of Your death and resurrection. Continue to teach me how to reflect your beauty so that I can bring beauty into being. In Jesus' name, Amen.

Activate by Restfully Making Things Happen

"Gentleness is strength under control. It is the ability to stay calm, no matter what happens." —Elizabeth George

God has given us bodies that respond to different sights, smells, and sounds. Write down the ones that bring beauty into being and cultivate a life of peace and rest. Maybe it's your favorite music. I love all types of music, especially classical and worship music. Create a playlist of your favorite music and make a plan for how you're going to incorporate your "peaceful pleasures of sound" into your daily routine and rest times. Make sure to schedule it into your planner.

Self-Care Task: Embrace your true beauty. Make a list of your greatest qualities, turn them into affirmations and read the list often.

DAY 18: BUILD A LIFE OF GRACE AND EASE

"Tea is the elixir of life." —Myoan Eisai

"Cast your cares on the LORD and he will sustain you; he will, never let the righteous be shaken" (Psalm. 55:22).

W e live in a world filled with temptations that lead to anxiety. Problems at work, at home, health issues, world events, pain from the past, or fear of the future—all can tempt us to worry.

We cannot know rest if we are constantly worried. We can't know calm and stillness if our mind is constantly thinking about paying bills, dealing with health problems, and evaluating the future. There is a time and place for these things, but they should not be constant themes in your life.

The Remarkable Woman, because of God's unconditional favor, knows how to cast all of her fears, worries, stressors, and anxieties on Him. She gains the ability to navigate and flow through life with greater freedom, refined by the "fire," poised and graciously ready to handle the next obstacle.

Ease doesn't mean easy. It does mean the burden you are carrying can be less painful and intense. And you tend to flow through the issues of life with a quiet state of mind. As a matter of fact, you can't carry these burdens yourself. If you try to, you'll end up exhausted, depleted, and burned out. Instead, God invites you to bring these burdens to Him.

What are you worried about? You can find rest by bringing these worries straight to God. He doesn't want you to constantly be worried and weighed down by the issues of life. Choose to live your best life with grace and ease. Experience the peace His unmerited favor brings knowing He loves you and has everything under control. Go ahead and let it go! **R**elease **E**very **S**ituation **T**otally.

Reflect and **Release Every Situation Totally**

1. Do you experience a lot of worry?
2. What are some things you are worried about, and why?
3. Will you commit to trusting the Lord afresh in a way that releases your worry to Him?

Tea Time and Conversation with God:

Lord, thank You that You have provided a way out of my worries and concerns. I desire to live a life of grace and ease. Please help me to take it to You rather than being burdened by concerns. Please help me to let go of worry and to consciously place my trust in You to take care of me. In Jesus' name, Amen.

Activate by Restfully Making Things Happen

The beginning of anxiety is the end of faith, and the beginning of true faith is the end of anxiety. —George Mueller

Look up the words "grace" and "ease." Put on your favorite peaceful music, grab a cup of tea, your favorite notebook or journal, and sit in your favorite spot. In your notebook, write down all the things that are currently causing you worry. Then, give each one of those things to God, trusting him to take care of them.

Self-Care Task: Take up yoga. Join a class at your local YMCA, gym, or online and relax. Yoga has been proven to reduce the impact that stress causes to your mind and body.

DAY 19: BUILD A LIFE OF VISION

Drink your tea slowly and reverently, as if it is the axis
on which the world earth revolves—slowly, evenly,
without rushing toward the future. —Thich Nat Hahn

"And the LORD answered me: 'Write the vision;
make it plain on tablets, so he may run who reads it' "
(Habakkuk 2:2 ESV).

*E*ye fatigue is real and can have a negative effect on your vision. Straining to see small objects, the computer screen, and continuously staring at a phone will place strain on your eyes.

Just as we must be intentional about preserving our physical vision, we must be intentional about clarifying our spiritual vision! Sharpen your vision so that you can see the future that God has in store for you.

There's nothing more frustrating than impaired vision. As someone who is extremely nearsighted, I know this discomfort all too well. Driving at night or during a storm can make it challenging to see the road ahead clearly.

Reading in a dimly lighted room can likewise put a strain on your eyes. In the same way, depression, sorrow, and the violent circumstances of life cloud our ability to see what the Lord has for us.

The vision for your Remarkable Life cannot be self-generated. Rather, it must come from God. It will require faith to achieve it especially when the road ahead seems dark and dim. So you need to seek Him for clarity to see it through His eyes. Wait on Him. Pause and slow your life down so that you can hear from the Lord. Grab a journal or a piece of paper and write what God is showing you.

Ask Him to show you the steps you need to take. It may not come to you right away; sometimes it takes time. Trust God to give you the plan. Rest and begin to see the vision more clearly. Dream. Then, write it down and connect it to His purpose for you and activate your life in His Spirit. We must be prepared to run with a clear focus. Strength will be required for the fulfillment of the vision. Rest continually so that you can enjoy the remarkable things happening in your life. Let's make sure to do so for His glory, with grace and ease.

God created us with a remarkable destiny in our future. In order to experience this destiny, we must live our lives with the end in mind. This requires having a clear vision of where we are headed and of what we are called upon to accomplish. Each day we must wake up with the purpose of making this vision a reality.

We are not here to live ordinary lives, but rather extraordinarily, Remarkable ones. Our intent is to live lives that reflect the God that we serve. Through the power of His presence we can accomplish things that are exceptional and worth the remark. This type of life is not easy, and there are costs. We must become comfortable with being known as unique, distinct, and perhaps even "peculiar."

When we embrace and reflect our God-given uniqueness, the contributions that we make will stand out above the noise. The attention we get serves as a reminder of the kind of impact we make, all because of being made in His image.

Our vision should be big, scary, and unforgettable and worth writing down and committing to memory. Our vision should make us excited every time we read or remember it, because it leads to a Remarkable Life that has meaning and significance.

God wants us to keep this vision in front of us so that we can see it clearly and without interruption. We should purposefully and consistently move toward it daily until it becomes a reality. It's not unusual that this vision is so big that it feels scary. Hence, as Remarkable Women God wants us to become alert, focused, refusing to play small, but rather praying and trusting Him to direct our lives even during the seasons of overwhelm. When we do, we can expect Him to provide the resources needed to make this remarkable vision a reality. Let's choose to see what He sees and begin today to restfully move towards it.

Reflect and **Release Every Situation Totally:**

1. What do you believe the Lord would have you specifically do with your life?
2. Do you have a plan in place for how this is going to happen, or are you still vague about things?
3. Are you regularly spending time in the Word to train your discernment and sensitivity to the Lord's plan?

Tea Time and Conversation with God:

Lord God, thank You for including me in Your plan for the world. Thank You that I have a specific part to play in how my life will turn out and in that great kingdom plan. Please give me clarity about my vision and how best to pour out my life in service to You, in a way that only I can. Teach me to trust You as I wait for that clarity and to not be idle but to serve You faithfully and joyfully until the clarity comes. In Jesus' name, Amen.

Activate by Restfully Making It Happen

The man doesn't make the vision; the vision makes the man. —Pastor Yonggi Cho

Rest your eyes for at least 10 minutes for every 50 minutes you are in front of a computer screen. Rest them through blocking out the light by cupping your hands and placing them over your eyes, or wearing a night mask perhaps in a print, such as an animal print, my favorite, or a design that reflects your life's vision statement. Making sure to get at least seven to eight hours of sleep a night also helps. Schedule this in your Rest and Build planner.

Self-Care Task: Create a vision board to help you stay focused. Using a form board or an online app, place words, images, and phrases to crystallize and convey the message of your vision.

DAY 20: BUILD A LIFE SEEKING GOD'S FACE

Strange how a teapot can represent at the same time
the comforts of solitude and the pleasures of company.
—Anonymous

And He said, "My presence shall go with you, and I will give
you rest" (Exodus 33:14 NASB).

My husband has traveled the majority of our married life speaking, consulting, and ministering. Many times when he was away, my nights were restless. There was nothing like his first night home, because by just being in his presence, seeing him face-to-face, I could finally get the rest that I so craved. His presence brought peace.

Moses, in the midst of leading in the wilderness, wanted the true peace that only the presence of God could provide. He had previous wilderness experience—working for his father-in-law, isolated on a mountain for 40 years where biblical scholars say there was no mention of the presence of God.

He wanted to place his confidence in the Almighty God, Jehovah Shamar—the God who is there, who provides. When God promised His presence, the word that was used meant "faces." God was promising to be with him in the journey, manifesting Himself as needed as if they were seeing His face.

In our journey to experiencing the Remarkable Life, our promised land, when we go through the wilderness-like experiences we must tap into His presence. When we do, it will inspire us to rest. In order to fulfill the purposes and plans of God, we must rest. But true, peaceful rest, especially in the midst of adversity and affliction, can't be experienced apart from His presence.

In the midst of confusion and chaos, He can provide grace and mercy!

Let's choose to become remarkable women of God who choose not to make this a casual expression, but rather live with this intimacy with Him that makes the enemy restless. Let's boldly tap into His presence so that the powerful confidence we exude comes from a restful place. We must refuse to move without seeing His face.

As you look at what you have in front of you, what must you do to invite the presence of God into your life? Watch the remarkable impact you will have on the world by building a life of seeking to see His face.

Reflect and Release Every Situation Totally

1. How can the knowledge that God is personally present with you today refresh, reassure, and encourage you?

2. Are there practical steps you can take to be more conscious that the Lord is present with you?

3. How do you imagine His face to appear? How can this bring you peaceful rest in your wilderness moments?

Tea Time and Conversation with God

Lord God of heaven, thank You that just as You were present with Israel of old in their wilderness wanderings, You are present with me, Your forgiven and dearly loved child. I want to see your face. Please help me to rest in the assurance, comfort, and accountability that Your holy presence brings. Teach me to trust You and Your provision. In Jesus' name, Amen.

Activate by Restfully Making Things Happen

The Lord watches over us every moment of every day. He is there—and He cares about every step and every breath. —Dillon Burroughs

One way to know that you're too hurried is to look at the way you eat. If you're constantly scarfing down your food without savoring it, you're probably rushing from one thing to the next. Prepare yourself a healthy, delightful meal or snack and set aside time to do nothing but eat, mindfully. Savor the moment. Imagine that you are dining in the presence of God, the Master Creative Designer. Savor looking into His face, feeling the rest that comes with peacefully eating and appreciating His provision. Imagine Him smiling as He watching you in delight.

Self-Care Task: Listen to inspiring podcasts on leadership, Christian growth, self-care, wellness, and personal development.

DAY 21: BUILD A LIFE OF LETTING GO

The most trying hours in life are between four o'clock and the evening meal. A cup of tea at this time adds a lot of comfort and happiness. —Royal S. Copeland

". . . casting all your anxiety on Him, because He cares for you" (1 Peter 5:7 NASB).

I don't particularly like to fish. Don't get me wrong, it is very relaxing being on the water. But it's the process of baiting, casting, and waiting, that I find to be the hardest.

It requires patience and practice. Take, for instance, casting, you have to know how to hold and use your rod. You also must be able to point it in the direction where you want your lure to go while pointing and releasing with accuracy. The key is to properly plant your foot, square your shoulders and find your target while flinging the rod in the direction you want it to go. Making sure that you have the right rod makes all the difference.

You can learn a lot about the Remarkable Life through fishing. In order for you to live your best Remarkable Life, you must learn the art of casting. You must learn to confidently square your shoulders, find your target—the cross—and start down the path towards HIM. He is waiting with open arms because of His great love and care for you.

We are called to build His Kingdom. In this life, you should expect trials and tribulations when it comes to Kingdom building, because they are part of what God uses to build in your heart and courage it takes to be a fisher of people. Having Christ as your rod makes the difference. Rest. Release. Let it go!

Reflect and Release Every Situation Totally

1. What are issues in your life that seem insurmountable and frightening to you? Name them and think about why they feel insurmountable.
2. Is it your habit to cast your anxieties and concerns onto the Lord, or do you cast them on yourself or keep them to yourself and try to be your own savior?
3. How are your trials being used by the Lord to teach you to rest and to make you a better fisher of people?

Tea Time and Conversation with God

Lord God, I praise You that in Your loving sovereignty, You have appointed trials in my life to teach me to exercise trust in You. Thank You for Your desire and interest to take upon Yourself my fears and anxieties. Please help me to release my anxieties to You as an act of faith and know Your strengthening and provision as You mature me through them. Thank You for being my rod. I'm ready to let making the cross my focus. In Jesus' name, Amen.

Activate by Restfully Making Things Happen

"Getting over a painful experience is much like crossing monkey bars. You have to let go at some point in order to move forward." —C. S. Lewis

Do you have a heart for the people? Are you aggressively looking for ways to build up the lives of others spiritually? Are the cares of life getting in the way? Our main purpose in life should be to know God and make Him known through our words and actions. Too often, we allow the cares of life to get in the way. Refuse to allow your challenges to prevent you from fulfilling this purpose. Make a list of the top five concerns you have. Pray thoroughly over them, releasing each one to the Lord's care and concern. Let it go!

Restful Sleep: Sleep is a Healthy Habit

Sleep is as important to your health as a healthy diet and regular exercise. The healthy habits of sleep, often called "sleep hygiene," are tips that can improve your ability to fall asleep and stay asleep.[8] These include establishing a relaxing bedtime routine, creating a soothing bedroom environment, and avoiding caffeine in the late afternoon and evening. For example, one study found that consuming caffeine six hours before bedtime reduced total sleep time by one hour.[9] You also should limit nighttime exposure to bright light from electronic devices such as tablets and smart-phones. This light sends an alerting signal to your brain that can delay the onset of sleepiness.[10]

Self-Care Task: Practice a random act of kindness. Get creative and let go of your inhibitions. Do something, unprovoked, because of Jesus' finished work on the cross on your behalf.

DAY 22: BUILD A LIFE OF ALIGNMENT

Better to be deprived of food for three days, than tea for one. —Chinese Proverb

"Better a dry crust with peace and quiet than a house full of feasting, with strife" (Proverbs 17:1 NASB).

G etting married can be easy; staying married can be more of a challenge. There are ebbs and flow. Although my goal was to build a home with laughter in the walls, there have been those days where it has been filled with unrest. How did *our* home, intended for feasting, become filled with strife? That was not the Remarkable Life of my dreams.

Even as ministry leaders, we have had seasons where we lost sight of our priorities due to busyness. Priorities are profoundly important. Often, problems and dissatisfaction come from not having the right priorities flowing out of a right worldview and value system. Most of us desire a rich life with perfect health, lots of money, beautiful home, a wonderful passion-filled marriage, and children who follow the path we set before them.

These are not wrong in themselves, and God does bless in these ways according to His will, but Proverbs 17 shows us that there are some things that money can't buy.

One of those things is peace! Which would you rather have: lots of stuff, but a warring, tense, ungodly family; or little in the way of material possessions and influence, but rest, joy, contentment, and happiness?

The answer should be obvious.

As you journey forward in building a Remarkable Life, from a place of grace and ease, God desires to teach you to have His priorities. He will seek to wean you away from wrong priorities sourced in the flesh and give you the values and emphases of the Spirit-filled life.

As you look to Him in faith, you will increasingly value what He does, and He will bring it to pass in your life.

When you operate according to God's priorities, you experience peace, joy, and rest. When you only operate out of your priorities, you will experience stress. The Remarkable Life comes, especially in relationships, when our priorities are in alignment with God's priorities.

Reflect and Release Every Situation Totally

1. Are there any areas in your marriage or other significant relationships where you might not have God's priorities in mind due to a lack of alignment?

2. Is your home filled with strife? How can rest move higher up on your priority list?

3. What is a practical step you can take to cultivate the Lord's priorities in your life and heart?

Tea Time and Conversation with God

Lord God, I know that Your ways are not my ways and Your thoughts not my thoughts. Because there is a gap between You and me, I will have a learning process to undergo as I grow in grace. Please illuminate my heart to areas in my marriage

or other relationships where I do not have Your priorities.
Give me the grace to change and learn from You. In Jesus'
name, Amen.

Activate by Restfully Making Things Happen

*It often happens that when couples get their
relationship to God straightened out, their
relationships with one another begin to straighten out
as well.* —Wayne Mack

Look at your marriage, family, or other close relationships. What is your vision for the future? What are God's priorities for you in each of those areas? Write those priorities down. Then write down *your* current priorities in those areas. If there are any differences between your priorities and God's, take them to God in prayer and ask for help to change. Think of activities that will help you make your family a priority.

Grab your planner and schedule a weekly date night with your husband or friend to continue to make a peaceful home a priority. Use the time to ask questions, prepared in advance, and engage in meaningful life-giving conversation.

***

Self-Care Task: Snuggle with your spouse, child, or furry pet.

DAY 23: BUILD A LIFE OF FOCUS

Tea is quiet and our thirst for tea is never far from our craving for beauty. —James Norwood Pratt

". . . And to make it your ambition to lead a quiet life and attend to your own business and work with your hands, just as we commanded you" (1 Thessalonian 4:11 NASB).

For many of us, our ambition in life is to find our dream job, make a certain amount of money, acquire things, and live a life of freedom. This is our picture of Remarkable Living. However, the Bible teaches us to intentionally aspire to lead a quiet, targeted, and focused life. We are to practice a life of boundaries. We must learn the power of saying 'no' unapologetically. If we try to be everything for everyone, we'll be stretched too thin, become overwhelmed, and sooner or later burn out.

This is another area where divine boundaries come into play. A "quiet" life is one of dignity and respectability, stability, endurance, grace, and fruitfulness. It is not boisterous, rude, overbearing, demanding, brash or bossy. Attending to your own business means not only working hard at your job, business, or ministry but not rudely pushing your way into others' lives and concerns. "Work with your own hands" means to be self-supporting, creative as you produce things yourself that can meet your needs and be of service to others.

God really wants you to live a life of focus on the right things which will matter, not only now but, in eternity. In order for this to happen, you need to have the right boundaries in place. You need to be focused on what God wants you to do, not what everyone else wants you to do. Rest and stillness allow us focus on what God has called us to do with our lives. And in the words of my mother, "Stay focused." Keep the main thing the main thing by learning to quiet down your life?

Reflect and Release Every Situation Totally:

1. What do you need to do to quiet your life? How can you intentionally bring calmness into the moment?
2. What boundaries must you put into place in order to accomplish this ambition?
3. What kind of work can you create that is a blessing to others and can potentially even meet your own financial needs?

Tea Time and Conversation with God

Lord Jesus, thank You that You desire me to be creative and to live a quiet, respectable life. Because You are the Creator, You have good works for me to do. Please help me to be at rest and be respectable as I go about these works. Help me not to envy the works You've given others, but to focus wholly on the works You've given me. In Jesus' name, Amen.

Activate by Restfully Making Things Happen

"The successful man is the average man, focused."
—Unknown

Remember coloring as a child? It's time to reconnect with your inner child. If you don't have the supplies, go to a craft or art store and purchase an adult coloring book along with a set of colored pencils (Prisma are my all-time favorites), markers, or crayons. Schedule a time to relax, get quiet, express your creativity, and color. Don't over think it. Practice your coloring technique, like shading and staying in the lines as you clear your mind and focus. This mindful activity will help you relieve stress, drive away negative emotions, and anxiety. Set your timer, let go and stay fully-present in this life-giving moment.

Self-Care Task: Have a "Just Say No Day." Say "No" today to any and all excessive demands placed on you by others, especially if it causes you to feel hurried, stressed, or lose sight of what matters most in life. Live a calm life in complete alignment by learning to say "no" unapologetically.

DAY 24: BUILD A LIFE OF HARMONY

"Listen, if you want peace you must learn to drink chai from an empty cup." —James Clavell

"Now I exhort you, brethren, by the name of our Lord Jesus Christ, that you all agree and that there be no divisions among you, but that you be made complete in the same mind and in the same judgment" (1 Corinthians 1:10 NASB).

Growing up, I lived in a home where there were frequent disagreements between my parents. As a result, it created a home where conflict was the norm. There were nights when the arguments were so loud that not only was it difficult to sleep, but they caused me to become anxious and fretful. I would wake up in a panic at the sound of noise in the night.

Having this experience helped shape my view of the value of conflict resolution and harmony. Living the Remarkable Life is about protecting and promoting unity in all of your relationships across the board. We cannot allow division to become the norm. We must look for opportunities to find common ground in our thoughts and judgment.

One of the places where division happens, but we cannot afford it, is in the church. God has brought many diverse people into His one church through His Son and wants His bride, *us,* to have proper love and concern for the other members of the Body.

Often, division arises from arrogance, pride, ignorance or an unhealthy, narrow focus on having our own way. While there are certainly some areas we cannot compromise, we must balance devotion to truth with devotion to unity. Hurt feelings, misunderstandings and lack of forgiveness can all create contexts where unity is ruptured. The way back to harmony, of course, is confession and repentance. Let's work to create environments in the body of peace where strife and unrest is not tolerated. The world needs to see us take a stand that promotes harmony. God will bless us, as we embody the life of a Remarkable Woman of harmony by seeking to maintain the unity of the Spirit in the bond of peace (Ephesians 4:3).

Reflect and **Release Every Situation Totally:**

1. What are areas of disunity in your life? Think about them. What has contributed to unrest in your relationships?

2. Do you have any friction in your relationships in the body of Christ? What practical steps can you take to restore unity?

3. What are ways you can pursue common ground with people with whom you disagree while not compromising the truth of God?

Tea Time and Conversation with God

Lord Jesus, thank You that one of the effects of your death and resurrection is that You unite where there is a lack of unity. Thank You that You came to heal the divisions that stem from our sin, pride, and unbelief. Please help me to pursue Godly unity, based in the truth, with the Body of

Christ. Please give me the grace to repent of any sin or pride where I have created friction or disunity between myself and my family or another believer. Thank You that one day all of Your people will be perfectly one with You and with each other. In Jesus' name, Amen.

Activate by Restfully Making Things Happen

Love is the only force capable of transforming an enemy into a friend. —Martin Luther King Jr.

Cultivate rest in your relationships. One of the best ways to promote relational unity is to invest time in building a value for healthy communication. Today, take time to engage in meaningful connections. Call or write a family member or friend and simply tell them how much you appreciate them. Tell them why you're grateful for them and how much they mean to you. Avoid asking for anything or expecting anything in return. And if there is a broken or strained relationship that's in need of healing or reconciliation, pray and take the lead. Reach out, pursue peace, and seek to build unity.

Self-Care Task: Plan an adult play date with a friend, perhaps over tea. Laugh and enjoy one another's company. Create what I call "virtual tea time connections." From the comforts of your home you can connect!

DAY 25: BUILD A LIFE OF VICTORY

"When the going gets tough, the tough go to tea."
—J. S. Devire

"And it will be in the day when the LORD gives you rest from your pain and turmoil and harsh service in which you have been enslaved" (Isaiah 14:3 NASB).

I remember the moment that I turned my life around again after living a life of rebellion early in my relationship with God. I felt bound by the desire to sleep with a guy with whom I was engaged, although I knew it was wrong and I was tired of feeling so convicted by my sin. I wanted to break free from this bondage, its consequences and live a life of victory.

I did not feel as though I could break free from compromising my Biblical convictions, without jeopardizing our relationship. While it eventually cost me my relationship with this man, my desire to experience the inner peace of the Lord that REST in Him provided was of greater value. Likewise, Israel was in captivity in Babylon due to their rebellion. Sin will always take you some place you never thought you would go.

Israel, God's covenant people, were in a place of sorrow, trouble, and hard work because of their rebellion to God. But God, the Master Creative Designer, full of grace and mercy, did not give up on them. Instead, He promised to give them rest in the midst of the pain and suffering caused by their rebellion towards Him. He was willing to patiently wait, restore their broken lives and deliver on His promise of REST. What a picture of victory!

Rebellion can lead us into a life of pain and bondage. The Remarkable Life is a bondage-breaking life. We were designed to live victoriously. If you are in Christ by faith, God has made a way for every bondage and stronghold to be broken. *"Sin shall not have dominion over you, for you are no longer under law but under grace"* (Romans 6:14 NIV). Do not let your failures to obey and your weakness in listening to the lies of your flesh distract you from the great power and victory that are available to you in Christ.

See them as sin, but do not be so preoccupied by your failures that you can't move forward. Rest comes when we stop giving into our sin and run to God for true happiness. He is the one who frees us from our struggles and gives us true Shalom-peace.

When we let our sinful desires rule us we are actually *forfeiting* the peace, joy, and rest that God has for us. If you are bound up today by a life of sin—turn and choose to pursue God's standard of excellence. Now that's really good news! You can be free in Christ! REST and walk in victory.

Reflect and Release Every Situation Totally

1. Are there any specific sins or rebellion you're having trouble overcoming?
2. When you sin, do you run toward God or away from him?
3. How would victory look, sound, and feel to you in the areas you mentioned?

Tea Time and Conversation with God

Lord Jesus, thank You that your work on the cross secures my victory over sin! Please help me to trust that Your blood covers every sin and that it is available to me the instant I repent. Instead of being preoccupied by my failings, help me to claim your power and victory that is available to me in the gospel. You have promised it, so please help me to believe it! In Jesus' name, Amen.

A ctivate by Restfully Making Things Happen

"You don't really know Jesus is all you need until Jesus is all you have." —Tim Keller

Read I John 1:9. One of the most peaceful things you can do is realize that all your sins and rebellion to God's ways of remarkable living, and failings have been paid for and you don't need to do anything else. You can rest in God. You can trust His forgiveness. You can release every situation totally and walk in victory before Him. One powerful way to experience this is by writing your sins down, as a way of confession, crossing them out and writing "forgiven forever" and "victory" on top of it.

Afterwards, take the list, tear it into tiny pieces and toss it into the trash. This is a picture of God's response when we agree by confession that we have sinned against Him. Take 10 minutes to create your I John 1:9 list. Follow the steps to victory mentioned. Light an aromatherapy candle, close your eyes, and meditate on the sweet aroma of forgiveness.

————————— ❦ —————————

Self-Care Task: Splurge—buy yourself something self-indulgent, affordable, and within budget . . . just because of the freedom forgiveness brings.

—————————

DAY 26: BUILD A LIFE OF WISDOM

Elixir of the ages. Tea makes us all sages." —Dharlene
Marie Fahl

"Behold, a son will be born to you, who shall be a man of
rest; and I will give him rest from all his enemies on every
side; for his name shall be Solomon, and I will give peace
and quiet to Israel in his days" (1 Chronicles 22:9).

When you die, how do you want to be remembered? What
is the word you want others to use to describe you? What
purpose did you fulfill? What kind of legacy did you leave
behind for others to understand and follow? Solomon, the son of
David, who was considered to be the wisest man in the Bible, was
given the charge to complete the building of God's temple. His
presence, perhaps, mirrored the meaning of his name which means
"peace." His purpose was clear. He was called to build the temple
according to the blueprint and plans of his father who had received
them from God. It's believed to have taken him approximately 14
years to complete this assignment. And they were to build it in complete silence—no noise was to be made by the tools being used.
Truly he was a man of rest!

He lived a full and productive life with a presence which was
distinct and memorable. He loved and served God wholeheartedly
and experienced the Remarkable Life—one of peace. Not only for

himself but for ALL of his enemies and the people of Israel experienced peace and quiet because of Solomon.

Like him, we should also desire to be described as a woman of rest. But it takes wisdom to learn to live and lead from a place of rest. One of the biggest steps toward wisdom is making the choice to completely find ways to seek a life of rest in God's eyes. Sometimes, this may require that you to build in silence. And it requires that you surrender your time, schedule, and ambitions to Him.

This doesn't mean you give them up or stop pursuing them, but it does mean that you change the way you do it. Instead of doing it fearfully or every waking minute, you trust God to make your Remarkable Life happen. In wisdom, you work from a peaceful presence and mindset rather than a fearful and frantic one.

Reflect and Release Every Situation Totally

1. Do you ever feel worthless or not valued?
2. How does knowing that you are an accepted child of God help you conquer those feelings of worthlessness?
3. What is the legacy you want to leave to the next generation—one of wisdom, rest, and confidence in the Lord or one of harried self-focus? What steps of wisdom can you take, practically, to do this today?

Tea Time and Conversation with God

Heavenly Father, thank You that I am fully accepted in Christ, I do not have to work to be accepted by You. Thank You that Your acceptance is the most important thing and that I have had it fully since I first trusted in Christ. Please forgive me for demanding the acceptance of people, or for looking to it rather than You. Please help me to be satisfied with your lavish welcome and to rest in it with great joy. In Jesus' name, Amen.

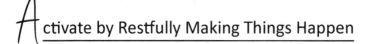

Activate by Restfully Making Things Happen

"We are made wise not by the recollection of our past, but by the responsibility for our future."
—George Bernard Shaw

One of the best ways to walk in wisdom, surrenderance to God, and rest is to intentionally stop working every day. Instead of constantly hustling and grinding, constantly working, trying to make things happen from our own strength. Stop, rest, and recharge. Surrender. Walk in wisdom. Try a technology fast for a designated period of time. Turn off your phone, stop answering emails don't engage on social media and simply be still. Do you have time for that in your day? If not, create a plan for when you will stop. Watch how God keeps things going and brings peace to your chaotic world while you rest.

Self-Care Task: Have electronic detox day— unplug all electronics for a designated period of time. Enjoy as you build in silence.

DAY 27: BUILD A LIFE OF SWEET SLEEP

"When I drink tea I am conscious of peace. The cool breath of heaven rises in my sleeves, and blows my cares away." —Lo Tung

"When you lie down, you will not be afraid; When you lie down, your sleep will be sweet" (Proverbs 3:24).

I magine sleeping in the most secure environment with a guard standing by, watching over you. It's likely that you would be able to sleep carefree, with no worries or anxieties. Sweet sleep should be the hallmark of the Remarkable Life and the life of a Remarkable Woman. It's a life of rest that brings about refreshment, restoration, and refinement.

God knows how to protect us from destruction, danger, or harm. Not only does He watch over you, but He will deliver you. REST requires that you release every situation totally and put your confidence in Him, completely. And knowing that He sees and watches us gives us the freedom to experience the sweet sleep of peace.

The presence of God promises to provide us with sleep. He is our confidence and He will not withhold any good thing from us. The Lord God is our keeper both day and night. He watches over us like a lover and protector, simply staring at us, gazing at our beauty while we are sleeping soundly in His arms.

Do you experience sweet sleep, or do you constantly fret, worry, and pace about through the night? Do you allow yourself time to unwind or do you stay up late working frantically until the last possible minute?

Sleep is a gift from God. When we sleep, we're saying to God, "I trust you to take care of all the things I can't." You can't have a Remarkable Life when you're grumpy, fuzzy-headed, and overwhelmed due to being sleep deprived. Adequate sleep and a Remarkable Life go hand in hand. Climb into His arms and . . . sleep. Don't miss out on the opportunity to REST in His presence.

Reflect and Release Every Situation Totally:

1. If you have difficulty sleeping because of anxiety, how can you apply the truth of God's personal watchful care to your worries?
2. How does the knowledge of God's personal presence with you during sleep help you put your anxieties in perspective?
3. What is a specific area where you would like to see God's deliverance? Ask Him for it.

Tea Time and Conversation with God

Heavenly Father, You are a gracious and tenderly compassionate God. Thank You for Your loyal love for me in Christ. Please help me to see and experience, by faith, the reality of Your personal protection of me, including during sleep. Help me to glorify You by believing what You said and living accordingly. In Jesus' name, Amen.

Activate by Restfully Making Things Happen

"True silence is the rest of the mind, and is to the spirit what sleep is to the body, nourishment and refreshment. "—William Penn

Spend time before bed in conscious meditation on Scripture and prayer to the Lord. In your journal, write down how you can apply the meaning of the text to your own life.

As adults, we are encouraged to get at least seven to eight hours of sleep at night. This won't happen without a plan and commitment to follow it. In your planner, schedule the time and make it a part of your self-care and evening rituals. Make it a goal to prepare yourself for bed at least one hour before bedtime. Begin slowing down and bringing things to a close one hour before bedtime, put on comfortable pj's, sip a cup of relaxing herbal tea such as chamomile. Shut off all electronics, adjust the room temperature, and dim the room lights. And, sleep well.

Self-Care Task: Before bed, using a diffuser, add essential oils, singularly or as a blend, that promote sweet sleep such as lavender, chamomile, bergamot, marjoram, or cedar wood. Fluff up your pillow, slip into bed and breathe in the air deeply, calmly, and enjoy sweet dreams!

DAY 28: BUILD A LIFE OF RESILIENCE

"Making tea is a ritual that stops the world from falling in on you." —Johnathan Stroud

"My flesh and my heart may fail, but God is the strength of my heart and my portion forever" (Psalm 73:26).

I will never forget the night when I felt like my heart was about to stop and I lost all sense of vitality. I'd just received news, from another friend, that a mutual friend I had mentored for years—who I had welcomed into my home, family, and deeper parts of my life—had made some hurtful and reckless comments about me and a family member and began turning others against me. It was devastating. And, I didn't have permission to talk with her.

I was not only dealing with the reality of the betrayal and its timing, but with the added pain of the heartless way the news was delivered. At that moment, I felt shame for being so trusting, vulnerable, by giving her that kind of access to the deeper parts of me and my life. This wasn't the first time I had experienced this kind of pain, but it felt like the final blow. I was exhausted by the betrayal and rejection. It caused me to question my own value and discernment abilities.

I began to travel back down a dark emotional road that had become all too familiar since high school. Questions begin to flood my mind. "Why am I here?" "Why does rejection always cut me so deeply?" "Why is my kindness constantly taken for granted?"

"Why can't I seem to shake this pain off?" I felt that others would be better off without me. Driving home after the conversation, I sobbed uncontrollably from the deepest parts of me. Pulling into my driveway, I still felt the urge to run away from the pain. I drove into my garage and with the car still running I pushed the remote to close the garage door. . . .

David, as mentioned previously, branded as a man after God's own heart, felt this kind of despair on many occasions. He was exhausted physically and emotionally by the constant pursuit of his unfaithful friends and enemies in his efforts to pursue God's guidance and maintain a love for his people as a leader. I'm convinced that he, too, struggled with suicidal ideations. But, it was during those times that he learned to REST in God which made Him the source of David's strength. As a result he learned how to build a life of resilience.

I'm grateful God gave me the strength to run to Him, push through another suicidal ideation and fight for my life. In that moment, the thoughts of my family and truth of the value of my presence snapped me back into reality. I'm grateful I had the resilience, on that night, to loudly blow the car horn until my husband came to my rescue. In tears I ran into his arms.

In this life, we will be overwhelmed by these issues if we don't learn to resist the urge to place our security in our circumstances, reputation, and abilities (always a sure recipe for disappointment in a fallen world). Instead we must learn to look to God, His purposes, promises, power, and His attributes as the only source of security. If we have Him, we have all we could ever need. With resilience we can be assured of a certain hope for today and tomorrow. Then and only then can we truly . . . REST.

Reflect and Release Every Situation Totally

1. How are you tempted to look to your abilities, circumstances, and reputation (or anything other than the Lord) for security?

2. Have you experienced betrayal at the hands of a close friend, mentee, church or family member? What does healing and forgiveness look like?

3. How can you apply the truth that the Lord Himself is your security to an issue you are facing today?

Tea Time and Conversation with God

Lord God, thank You that because of Your work in Your Son, You alone are my perfect sufficiency and security. Thank You that I have great hope in You as I face the wounds and trial of this fallen world. I know that even when relationships go wrong, You are always faithful to me. You love me and will never leave me or forsake me. Help me to rest in my constant, never failing relationship with You. In Jesus' name, Amen.

Activate by Restfully Making Things Happen

"Is it possible to succeed without any act of betrayal?"
—Jean Noir

Few things will keep you from wholeheartedly living the Remarkable Life like bitterness and grudges. They sour the spirit and keep you from being vibrant and radiant. One simple, yet powerful way to overcome grudges is to actually pray that God would bless the people who have hurt you. This doesn't mean that the pain isn't real or that what they did doesn't matter. It simply means that you're letting your relationship with God define you rather than the pain caused by someone else. Today, take at least five minutes to pray for someone who has hurt you. Drink deeply from the overflowing cup of life, sweetened with rest, which allows you to speak blessings over their life instead of curses.

Sleep is Essential for Optimal Health

The American Academy of Sleep Medicine recommends that adults should sleep seven or more hours per night on a regular basis to promote optimal health.[11] Sleeping less than seven hours nightly increases your risk of a variety of health problems. These include weight gain and obesity, type 2 diabetes, high blood pressure, heart disease, stroke, and depression. Insufficient sleep also increases your risk of drowsy driving, which takes the lives of thousands of people each year in the U.S.[12] Ultimately, people who sleep fewer than seven hours per night have a higher risk of death. Because of genetic factors, some people need less sleep than others. A small percentage of people are "short sleepers" who function normally on less than 6 hours of regular sleep.[13] However, most people who restrict their sleep to fewer than 7 hours per night are simply depriving themselves of the sleep they need. Data from the Centers for Disease Control and Prevention show that 35% of U.S. adults fail to sleep at least seven hours per night.[14] In recognition of the importance of sleep to health and well-being, and in response to the high prevalence of insufficient sleep, the CDC has called insufficient sleep "a public health problem."[15]

Self-Care Task: Get a facial or massage. Make an appointment to scrub away those dead cells or relax those tense muscles.

DAY 29: BUILD A LIFE OF WORSHIP

"I must drink lots of tea or I cannot work. Tea unleashes the potential which slumbers in the depth of my soul." —Leo Tolstoy

"There yet remains a Sabbath rest for the people of God" (Hebrews 4:9 ESV).

In the Old Testament, the Sabbath was God's appointed day of rest for the people of Israel. Rest was so important to God that He actually commanded the people of Israel to take a day off! This is how much God cares about our rest!

The idea of taking a day of Sabbath is incredibly powerful and can truly lead to a Remarkable Life. When we take a Sabbath, we are saying to God, "I trust you to take care of all the little details of my life. You are my provider. You are more than enough. I trust you to help me achieve my Remarkable Life even when I'm resting."

Our Sabbath is a time to contemplate, celebrate, create, and prepare ourselves to contribute even more to building not only our lives, but God's kingdom. This requires an extended period to rest.

When we take a Sabbath, it's also a reminder that Jesus has already accomplished everything for our salvation. We don't need to work to earn anything from God; Jesus did it all. When we know that, we can truly, deeply rest. We can enjoy the presence of God without feeling like we have to work our way in. We can have peace that passes all understanding.

Walking in His peace, regardless of our circumstances, shapes us into being seen, known, and remembered as Remarkable Women, restfully on the path that leads to a Remarkable Life in worship to Him.

Reflect and **Release Every Situation Totally:**

1. Do you take time for a "Sabbath" rest each week?
2. What things keep you from making adequate time for rest?
3. How does knowing God will meet all your needs encourage you to make space for rest?

Tea Time and Conversation with God

Father, thank You that in Christ You offer me rest and refreshment. Thank You that to know You is to know peace, contentment, blessing, and joy from the one true God and most glorious being in the universe. Thank You that I don't have to earn anything from You, but can simply enjoy the rest I have in Christ. Help me to stop constantly striving and grinding and to simply enjoy rest in You as my worship. In Jesus' name, Amen.

Activate Restfully Making Things Happen

The busyness of things obscures our concentration on God . . . Never let a hurried lifestyle disturb the relationship of abiding in Him. This is an easy thing to allow, but we must guard against it. —Oswald Chambers

Pull out your planner and schedule mini-Sabbath rest breaks, preferably daily, when you will do nothing but rest. This doesn't have to involve sleep, it simply means you cause things to stop. Pause. Unlike your weekly, extended Sabbath, typically on Sundays, this is a power pause to refresh you. The key is to stop your work, and rest in His presence, remembering that He is the one who sustains you.

Self-Care Task: Create a special hour of prayer. Spend time praying through the scriptures, hymnals and listening to worship music.

DAY 30: BUILD A LIFE OF CONNECTEDNESS

Where there's tea, there's hope. —Arthur Wing Pinero

"I have told you these things, so that in me you may have peace. In this world you will have trouble. But take heart! I have overcome the world" (John 16:33).

We will never fully escape the troubles and trials of this world. No matter how successful we are, there will always be challenges in our lives. We will always face some measure of struggle and frustration. That's simply what it means to live in this fallen world.

But, that doesn't mean that God doesn't want you to live your Remarkable Life. In fact, God has made a way for you to live a Remarkable Life even when you're facing struggles in challenging times. I learned this truth during the untimely and unexpected losses of my father (who I fondly referred to as "Daddy-O") and my only niece, Lauren, whose deaths were about a year apart, while I was in the midst of private persecution. The power for the Remarkable Life comes from Jesus. He has overcome the world, and through him we can also overcome the world. Only through staying connected to Him could I survive as a Remarkable Woman considering what I was going through at the time.

We can have peace when we are closely connected to Jesus. He is the source of peace and joy even when the storms are raging around us. He is the foundation of the Remarkable Life, and when we are close to Him we truly can fulfill God's purpose—even in our darkest moments in life.

There were many times when Jesus' disciples were afraid. However, when Jesus was present with them, there was nothing that could stand against them. You have Jesus present with you, and there's nothing that can stand against you! He gives you the power to be a Remarkable Woman even when you are afraid.

That's the secret to a Remarkable Life!

Reflect and Release Every Situation Totally

1. What are some of the current struggles you are facing?
2. What does staying connected to Him look like?
3. How does knowing that Jesus has overcome the world encourage you?

Tea Time and Conversation with God

Lord Jesus, thank You for the completeness and certainty of Your victory over this fallen world. Thank You for calling me out of the world to be Your disciple. Please help me to stay closely connected to You. Help me to stop trying to do things in my own strength and to always rely on Your strength. In Jesus' name, Amen.

Activate Restfully Making Things Happen

"A believer may pass through much affliction, and yet secure very little blessing from it all. Abiding in Christ is the secret of securing all that the Father meant the chastisement to bring us." —Andrew Murray

The best ways to stay closely connected to Jesus are through prayer and His Word. The challenge is to set aside time for those things. Schedule it in your planner. Prayer walk—reciting ABC prayers where you choose an adjective that describes God based on each letter of the alphabet. Don't be afraid to get creative by creating a prayer calendar. Today, make a cup of your favorite tea, get your Bible, and go to a still place. Spend time enjoying your tea, reading the Bible and praying for the things that are troubling you. REST and enjoy the peace that only He provides.

Self-Care Task: Connect with your creativity. Find a hobby or reconnect with a hobby. Schedule intentional leisure time to create and enjoy.

DAY 31: BUILD A LIFE OF MINDFULNESS

All true tea lovers not only like their tea strong, but like it a little stronger with each year that passes.
—George Orwell

"You will keep Him in perfect peace, whose mind is stayed on you, because He trusts in you" (Isaiah 26:3 ESV).

We have come to the end of our devotional look at designing and building a Remarkable Life, restfully. Hopefully, for you the journey is just beginning as you learn to better pursue Christ and rest in His perfect plan and provision for your life.

Remember, God doesn't want you to live a life of frantic hurry and anxiety. His will for you doesn't include burnout, overwhelming anxiety, or constant exhaustion. Rather, He wants you to slow down, have perfect peace, and fully enjoy being in the moment.

And the secret to this perfect peace is keeping your mind fixed on God and refusing to miss out on life due to being distracted or busy. This is mindfulness. Unlike when you're busy and worried, your mind is darting in a thousand different directions, trying to process everything, running at a thousand miles an hour. In contrast, the mind that is fixed on God is still and at peace. This is not the life for which you have been created and to live. You were designed to live a restful, refreshing and rewarding life.

When things are going well, fix your mind on God. REST. Stay right there in His presence. Look up and see His beauty. When you're struggling, fix your mind on God. REST. When you're feeling great, fix your mind on Jesus. REST. When you're in the dumps, keep your mind focused in the same place. Stay right there and fully embrace and be mindful of His presence. Look up and see His beauty.

Slow down and drink deeply from the cup of life. Enjoy being in the moment as you allow your life to center around being in His presence. May you continue to **R**elease **E**very **S**ituation **T**otally. I'm so excited to see how God is going to work in you to build an amazing, powerful, Remarkable Life. Make a commitment to daily live by design and not by default, with grace and ease. Refuse to go at it alone. This is just the beginning for you!

Here's to your best Remarkable Future!

Reflect and Release Every Situation Totally

1. What does it look like to keep your mind fixed on God?
2. When you're worried, what does your mind do?
3. How can you regularly remind yourself to keep your mind fixed on God in all circumstances?

Tea Time and Conversation with God

Lord, thank You that You give peace to me when I fix my mind on You. Help me to constantly focus my thoughts on who You are, what You can do, and how wonderful You are. Forgive me for all the times I let my mind wander about in worry. Thank You for the peace You promise! In Jesus' name, Amen.

Activate Restfully Making Things Happen

The Christian needs to walk in peace, so no matter what happens they will be able to bear witness to a watching world. —Henry Blackaby

Centering yourself is simply the practice of being mindful about where you are, your experiences, thoughts, and feelings and where they're leading you. When you're worried or fearful, you need to center your mind back on God. A simple way to practice mindfulness in this situation is to ask yourself, "What am I worried about?" Breathe, connect with your body, senses, thoughts, and experience. Breathe. Focus your attention on your present situation and experience. Own it. Become fully aware, acknowledge and embody it.

Then ask, "What does God say about that?" Again, breathe. Focus your attention on your present situation and experience. Connect with His presence. REST. Stay in the moment, fully aware and present. Become fully aware of His presence and voice, acknowledge what He is saying to you and embody it. Own it. REST. Stay in the moment. When you do these things, you'll see your worries begin to evaporate in God's presence.

Self-Care Task: Clear your mind from all mental blocks. Free yourself from regret. Forgive yourself for past mistakes and failures. Seize the moment to celebrate this life you are living that matters now and for an eternity. Enjoy a sweet treat.

ENDNOTES

1   Goel N, Basner M, Rao H, Dinges DF. "Circadian Rhythms, Sleep Deprivation, and Human Performance". Prog Mol Biol Transl Sci. 2013; 119: 155–190, https://www.ncbi.nlm.nih.gov/pmc/articles/PMC3963479/.

2   Wittmann M1, Dinich J, Merrow M, Roenneberg T. "Social Jetlag: Misalignment of Biological and Social Time". Chronobiol Int. 2006;23(1-2):497-509, https://www.ncbi.nlm.nih.gov/pubmed/16687322.

3   World Health Organization, "Mental health in the workplace" 2017 Sept. https://www.who.int/mental_health/in_the_workplace/en/

4   Luyster FS; Strollo PJ; Zee PC; Walsh JK. "Sleep: A Health Imperative". SLEEP 2012;35(6):727-734, https://www.ncbi.nlm.nih.gov/pmc/articles/PMC3353049/.

5   Xie L, Kang H, Xu Q, et al. "Sleep Drives Metabolite Clearance from the Adult Brain". Science 2013;342(6156):373-377, http://science.sciencemag.org/content/342/6156/373.

6   de Vivo L, Bellesi M, Marshall W, et al. "Ultrastructural Evidence for Synaptic Scaling Across the Wake/Sleep Cycle". Science 2017;355(6324):507-510, http://science.sciencemag.org/content/355/6324/507.

7   Holth J, Patel T, Holtzman DM. "Sleep in Alzheimer's Disease - Beyond Amyloid". Neurobiol Sleep Circadian Rhythms. 2017 Jan; 2:4-14, https://www.ncbi.nlm.nih.gov/pubmed/28217760.

8   American Academy of Sleep Medicine. "Healthy Sleep Habits". Updated Feb. 9, 2017, http://www.sleepeducation.org/essentials-in-sleep/healthy-sleep-habits.

9   Drake C, Roehrs T, Shambroom J, Roth T. "Caffeine Effects on Sleep Taken 0, 3, or 6 Hours Before Going to Bed". J Clin Sleep Me"d 2013;9(11):1195-1200, http://www.aasmnet.org/JCSM/ViewAbstract.aspx-?pid=29198.

10   Chang AM, Aeschbach D, Duffy JF, Czeisler CA. "Evening Use of Light-emitting eReaders Negatively Affects Sleep, Circadian Timing, and Next-morning Alertness". Proc Nat'l Acad Sci U S A. 161 2015;112(4):1232-1237, http://www.pnas.org/content/112/4/1232.full.

11   Watson NF, Badr MS, Belenky G, Bliwise DL, Buxton OM, Buysse D, Dinges DF, Gangwisch J, Grandner MA, Kushida C, Malhotra RK, Martin JL, Patel SR, Quan SF, Tasali E. "Recommended Amount of Sleep for a Healthy Adult: A Joint Consensus Statement of the American Academy of Sleep Medicine and Sleep Research Society". J Clin Sleep Med 2015;11(6):591–592, http://www.aasmnet.org/jcsm/ViewAbstract.aspx?pid=30048.

12   Watson NF, Morgenthaler T, Chervin R, Carden K, Kirsch D, Kristo D, Malhotra R, Martin J, Ramar K, Rosen I, Weaver T, Wise M. "Confronting Drowsy Driving: The American Academy of Sleep Medicine Perspective". J Clin Sleep Med 2015;11(11):1335–1336, http://www.aasmnet.org/jcsm/ViewAbstract.aspx?pid=30315.

13   American Academy of Sleep Medicine. International Classification of Sleep Disorders, 3rd Ed. Darien, IL: American Academy of Sleep Medicine,

2014, https://tinyurl.com/ya7ru9c2.

14   Liu Y, Wheaton AG, Chapman DP, Cunningham TJ, Lu H, Croft JB. "Prevalence of Healthy Sleep Duration among Adults"—United States, 2014. MMWR Morb Mortal Wkly Rep. 2016 Feb 19;65(6):137-41, https://www.cdc.gov/mmwr/volumes/65/wr/mm6506a1.htm.

15   Centers for Disease Control and Prevention. National Center for Chronic Disease and Prevention and Health Promotion, Division of Adult and Community Health. "Insufficient sleep is a public health problem". Updated Sept. 3, 2015, https://www.cdc.gov/features/dssleep/.

Thank you for slowing down to spend your precious time embarking on this journey over a cup of tea. This is a *grace and ease* movement of Remarkable Women who dare to *rest and build* their best, remarkable life by God's design.

And, it doesn't have to end here.

Let's stay connected!

Here are three quick and easy ways to do just that:

1. Join my mailing list and get a FREE Checklist: *30 Ways to Live Your Best Remarkable Life with Grace and Ease* at: https://remarkablelivinginstitute.com/free.

2. Join Remarkable Life By Design, a membership community, to continue the journey and on-going teaching and support. Visit: www.remarkablelivinginsitute.com/joinRLBD and join us.

3. Visit Facebook and join the private group, Grace and Ease Living Sisterhood for daily tips, inspiration, engagement, events, and updates on new product releases.

For speaking engagements or more information email: info@remarkablelivinginstitute.com.

Your thoughts matter! Please share your review on Amazon at: https://www.amazon.com/dp/B07QMZWSWD/.

CPSIA information can be obtained
at www.ICGtesting.com
Printed in the USA
LVHW081714121120
671523LV00038B/1163